ANCIENT ROME
ON FIVE DENARII A DAY

The emperor Marcus Aurelius enters Rome in triumph.

PHILIP MATYSZAK

ANCIENT ROME
ON FIVE DENARII A DAY

with 43 illustrations, 11 in color

CONTENTS

GETTING THERE

Puteoli · Hitting the Road

ALL ROADS, THEY SAY, LEAD TO ROME. But choose carefully which road to take, and just as importantly, when to take it. Go too early, and you will struggle against winter storms. Go too late, and all the festivals and spectacles will have finished, and everyone who can will have fled the summer heat to the seaside resort of Baiae, or the cool of the Tuscan hills. Really late arrivals will be just in time for the first damp of autumn – the unhealthiest time of year in an eternally unhealthy city.

In short, the journey must be carefully planned. The more organized the traveller, the fewer nasty surprises during the journey. *Festina lente*, 'hurry slowly', the Romans say, and it is good advice. Where are you going to stay? How will you pay? What types of transport are available? The answers may come as a surprise. The Roman world is two thousand years away, but it is still surprisingly sophisticated.

Make a start as soon as possible by organizing somewhere to stay in Rome. Do this by offering lodgings and hospital-ity to a Roman visiting your city. The Romans are great travellers, and are as keen (or keener) to save a *denarius* as anyone else. They also have a strong sense of obligation amounting to a moral code, and once ties of guest-friendship (*hospitium*) have been forged with a Roman visitor, he will almost certainly leave behind an invitation to stay with him should you come to Rome. This is why any visiting Roman of any importance has people almost falling over themselves to offer food and shelter. The relatively minor inconvenience of putting up a guest for a while is one of the best ways of ensuring roughly equivalent accommodation on a return visit to the imperial city.

Staying in Rome is not cheap, and the journey itself is going to be expensive. While the central areas of the empire are well policed and the roads generally safe from brigands, many petty thieves and riff-raff consider travellers easy prey.

Most Roman travellers carry their money in a bag around their necks, or in a belt on their waists. It is a good idea to

> *We were happy to get here, and happier yet to depart*
> *We want to see Rome again, and our own household gods*
>
> GRAFFITO FROM POMPEII,
> *CIL* 4.1227

carry only the minimum amount of money required for the journey, and collect the rest in Rome.

The procedure for this is as follows. All major shipping associations and merchant houses have offices abroad, and some commercially minded cities have representatives scattered about the empire to look after the welfare and business interests of their travelling citizens.

Find one of these businesses which has offices in Rome, and give them the money that you intend to spend in the Eternal City. For an agreed percentage (don't forget to haggle this down!) their representative will hand over a receipt which can be changed back into money at their offices in Rome. This reduces the amount that has to be carried on the journey, and saves the trouble of changing the coins into Roman currency on arrival (see **Changing Money** p. 66).

Bring your gold jewelry with you but keep it well out of sight

A ROMAN SOLDIER WRITES TO HIS WIFE BEFORE HER VISIT

To speed up the journey and save on overnight accommodation, it is best to do the first leg by sea, to the port of Puteoli in Campania, a few days' journey south of Rome. Talk to the shipping agents at the nearest large seaport to arrange this voyage. The optimum choice would be in the early spring on a merchant ship with cargo for Capua. For a quicker journey, look for a grain ship bound for Rome's seaport of Ostia, though this option means missing the experience of a journey up the Appian Way, arguably the most famous of all ancient roads.

Apart from the occasional ferry across the Adriatic, passenger boats do not exist. However, most merchant ships accept passengers, and using a good shipping agent means that an unscrupulous captain won't help himself to your possessions before dropping you overboard once well out to sea. Piracy has diminished considerably since its heyday during the last years of the Roman Republic, but not every ship is beyond reproach!

Once a departure date has been fixed, depending on where you live, an exit visa might be needed. Check carefully how much this will cost. In the east of the empire, for example, prices range from 8 to 108 drachmas depending on the person and how valuable the governor's office thinks that person is to the local economy. (As always with imperial bureaucracy, having a well-placed 'friend' can make these little problems go away, so enquire – delicately – how much making such a friend might cost.)

Take your own provisions for the journey. The ship's captain will supply water for cooking and drinking, and if asked nicely, or paid extra, might allow access to the ship's galley where travellers or their servants can prepare meals. The chart on the next page shows the minimum times for a sea voyage; though unfavourable winds and weather can easily make the trip much longer, or cause it to finish unexpectedly somewhere completely different.

Mention a sea voyage to a Roman, and the reaction will probably include a hiss of indrawn breath and a sad shaking of the head. The Romans are natural landlubbers who take to the water with deep reluctance and the gloomy conviction that it is the last thing they will ever do. The abundant ancient shipwrecks littering the Mediterranean seabed prove that for many this was indeed the case. Travellers might care to peruse the hilarious sea voyage in Petronius' *Satyricon*, and the less amusing fate of this would-be voyager...

When searching for contraband they [customs officers] rip up bags and packages. The law permits this, and it is not a good idea to try to stop it

PLUTARCH, *MORALS: ON CURIOSITY*

A human body was driving ashore, tossing lightly up and down on the waves. I stood sadly waiting, gazing with wet eyes on the work of the faithless element, and soliloquized, 'Somewhere or another, perhaps, a wife is looking in blissful security for this poor fellow's return, or a son perhaps, or a father, all unsuspecting of storm and wreck; be sure, he has left someone behind, whom he kissed fondly at parting. This then is the end of human projects, this the accomplishment of men's mighty schemes. Look how he now rides the waves!'

PETRONIUS, *SATYRICON* 115

Despite such grim sentiments, sea travel in this period flourishes to a degree not seen again for well over a millennium. The supertankers of the day are the huge ships from Alexandria, each capable of carrying one or two hundred passengers and 350 tonnes of Egyptian grain. Most travellers sail on something more modest – on ships like the *Europa*, a cargo vessel depicted in the plaster of a house in Pompeii. It is about 70 feet long, with a high stern and prow. Powered by a large square-rigged sail, it is steered by an oar at the

MINIMUM TIMES FOR A SEA VOYAGE

Route	Miles	Days
Rhegium – Puteoli	175	1.5
Africa – Ostia	270	2
Carthage – Syracuse	260	2.5
Tauromenium (Sicily) – Puteoli	205	2.5
Massilia (Marseilles) – Ostia	380	3
Spain (northern) – Ostia	510	4
Alexandria – Ephesus (in Greece)	475	4.5
Corinth – Puteoli	670	4.5
Alexandria – Messina (Sicily)	830	6, 7
Carthage – Gibraltar	820	7
The Pillars of Hercules (Gibraltar) – Ostia	935	7
Alexandria – Puteoli	1000	9

Merchant ship coming to harbour at Portus, a few miles from Ostia on a branch of the Tiber. The letters VL on the sail stand for Votum Libero ('Dedicated by the Freedman'), and the crew are sacrificing in gratitude for the safe arrival of themselves and their cargo. Neptune stands on the dock with his trident.

back. The only living quarters on the ship belong to the captain. Passengers, like the slaves who make up the crew, sleep on deck.

No sane captain undertakes a voyage between 12 November and 10 March. This is the time of the *mare clusum* (the 'closed sea'), when winter storms make sea travel too dangerous to contemplate. Indeed, unless on truly urgent business, it is safer to wait until at least 27 March. In fact, since it is bad luck to be on the water at the end of any month, the journey will probably begin early in April. Then, if the captain has taken special care with the ritual sacrifice that precedes any lengthy sea voyage, the ship may be blessed with an Etesian wind, the gentle breeze that speeds commerce about the Mediterranean during the sailing season.

PUTEOLI

PUTEOLI WAS ONCE THE PRINCIPAL PORT of Italy. A hundred years ago, Puteoli and the Greek island of Delos (a huge slave trading centre) were actually the major ports of the Mediterranean. Puteoli does a good trade in pottery and fabrics, but is mainly famous for its 'pozzoli' earth, a major ingredient of that miraculous building material, concrete, which the Romans are the first to use to its full potential, and which they make to a slightly higher standard than the 21st-century product.

On arrival, the attentions of the customs officers at the harbour must be endured. Like revenue officers in all times and places, Roman customs men make up in official powers what they might lack in courtesy.

At least Puteoli is a Roman port – landing in a nominally non-Roman area, such as Tarentum or Naples, means that your luggage is violated once by local officials, and again on entry into 'Roman' territory.

Arriving on a *dies nefastus*, a day when the markets are officially closed, will delay the organization of the onward journey. (A *dies nefastus* is often the anniversary of an unfortunate incident – for example 18 July, when the Gauls chopped up a Roman army in about 390 BC.) Use any free time in Puteoli to visit the splendid amphitheatre. This is 489 by 381 feet, and has an arena of 245 by 138 feet. The tyrant emperor Nero is believed to have taken part in the games here, though the present structure dates to the Flavian dynasty which succeeded him. Among other points of interest are the town's aqueducts, one of which will still be bringing water to the city 2,000 years later.

But perhaps after a rather cramped sea voyage, the first stop should be Puteoli's *thermae*, the public baths, fed from a local spring. Afterwards, suitably groomed and sweet-smelling, proceed towards the large statue of the god Serapis which presides over the local market, situated conveniently near the docks, there to arrange the next stage of the journey.

HITTING THE ROAD

DON'T EXPECT TO TRAVEL THE ROADS in comfort. Sprung suspensions are almost non-existent, and most vehicle axles have a mere handful of fat to allow them to turn on their bearings. The squeal of badly greased axles will be a constant companion along the roads to Rome (though heavy carts are not allowed to enter the city itself during the day). Horses are rare, and generally used only by the imperial post and the army, and are not particularly comfortable anyway, given the rudimentary Roman saddles and total lack of stirrups (which won't arrive in Italy for another few centuries). However those who choose to walk, as many do, might obtain a donkey to carry the luggage.

If travelling as a couple, consider a *birota*, which as the name suggests (*bi rota* means 'two wheels') is a light and relatively speedy two-wheeler – the nearest most travellers will get to a chariot. These (often fantastically ornamented) sports cars of antiquity are more often rich kids' toys than serious people-carriers. A travelling family should consider a *carruca dormitoria*, a large covered waggon in which everyone can sleep, so saving the cost of staying overnight at an inn.

The very rich will want a litter, or at least a sedan chair, carried in relays by four to eight slaves, with a footman clearing the peasants from the road before them. Early in the Roman Republic, litters were considered suitable only for the sick and the seriously degenerate, but lately this mode of transport has become more acceptable.

The Appian Way was the first of the great Roman roads which are now a wonder of the empire. No civilization before has produced a road network of such size. Other roads follow the terrain, often following ancient footpaths, but the meticulously surveyed Roman roads run arrow-straight across the landscape, spanning marshes and cutting through hills. In fact one such cutting where the emperor Trajan extended the Appian Way along the coast is 120 feet deep.

All Roman roads are built to the same formula – a broad trench about four feet deep is filled with a solid foundation of sand and rubble. Then comes a layer of compacted gravel and clay, topped off with flagstones, carefully cambered to allow rainwater to run off to the sides. After all this, it is something of a let-down to discover that most vehicles do not travel on the road itself. Very few animals in antiquity are shod, and to save the animals' hooves most vehicles travel on the verge, leaving the road free for pedestrians.

Progress toward Rome is marked by regular milestones (the Roman mile is 95 yards shorter than the later measurement of that name). The milestones – round or oval stone posts – often give extra information such as who built or maintained that stretch of road. Particularly prolix milestones stand side by side to hold all the extra detail. At other times the stones occur only every league (a Roman *leuga* is 1.5 miles). When in Rome itself, be sure to seek out the famous Golden Milestone in the Forum. This is actually a marble column erected by the emperor Augustus which is covered with bronze plaques giving the distances to the cities of Rome's empire.

Maps are generally in the form of a band representing the points along the journey – they do not give general topographical information, or points of the compass.

Tombs line the Appian Way, a busy commuter route, outside Rome. Many of these houses of the dead are the size of apartment blocks – for example, the massive round tomb of Caecilia Metella in the background is 36 feet high with a diameter of 96 feet.

Three silver cups (later displayed in the Kircherian Museum in Rome) have distances and way stations engraved on them for the journey from Gades (Cadiz) to Rome. Most maps will list the imperial way stations (*mansiones*), which keep a change of vehicles and horses for those on imperial business, but which also offer food and accommodation to the general traveller.

Mansiones appear every dozen miles or so, and if accommodation is not available in these, there are alternatives. A *stabulum* is a sort of motel, with overnight stabling for animals and hospitality within. A funerary inscription in Aesernia in central Italy gives an excellent description of the facilities on offer:

> '*Innkeeper, the bill please!*'
> '*You had a pint of wine, one* as *[a shilling's worth] of bread and three* asses *of sauce*'
> '*Correct*'
> '*You had a girl for eight* asses'
> '*That's right*'
> '*And two* asses *of hay for your mule*'
> '*That damn animal is going to ruin me!*'

The best class of overnight accommodation is a *hospitium*, though even there expect the furnishing to be sparse. Travellers must share their accommodation with as many people as the landlord can cram in, and with a goodly number of bedbugs too. If travelling on the cheap, choose a *caupona* and share with the local ne'er-do-wells and a lower class of bedbug. Also, ask around for private houses which take overnight guests. One such house has a plaque which states pithily, 'If you are clean and neat, you'll find a room waiting for you here. If you're a slob, well, I blush to say it, but you are welcome as well.'

Remember to keep a keen eye on your property in these rooms. Innkeepers and ship's captains are responsible by law for possessions which go astray (though many display signs denying liability for coinage or jewelry), but the owners of private rooms are not.

The other travellers on the road are a mixed bag. Despite the hazards of travel, the Romans take to the roads in great numbers. There is a thriving tourist industry, not only of people visiting Rome, but sons of the wealthy doing grand tours of Greece or Egypt (and scratching their graffiti onto the monuments for later visitors to view).

Many people set out on pilgrimages seeking an oracle or to pray for their health at famous shrines, returning home refreshed and invigorated – though perhaps exercise and fresh country air bestow as much good as the deity. Businessmen and merchants are constantly on the move, some with cages of exotic animals, either for display or death in the insatiable Roman circuses (see **Entertainment** p. 80). There are local traders, following a circuit of towns according to the pattern of the

Some go on purposeless journeys, wandering up and down the coast, a morbid restlessness afflicts them no matter where they are, whether travelling by sea or land

SENECA, *ON PEACE OF MIND* 2.13

markets (most rural towns do not have shops, but hold markets at regular intervals). Some travellers are soldiers going or returning from leave, or acting as couriers, or on logistical duties. So many non-citizen soldiers (called *peregrini*) arrive in Rome that special quarters have been set aside for them. Among these soldiers was the centurion who brought St Paul to Rome. Any Roman citizen can, like St Paul, use the *Lex Iulia de Appellatione* to present his case personally to Caesar in Rome, and many do so.

The poet Horace travelled down the Appian Way, and some extracts from his diary give an impression of his journey (these extracts have been reversed since Horace travelled in the opposite direction):

This day we managed over 24 miles in our carriages.We spent the night in a town which I will not name in my verse, though I can easily

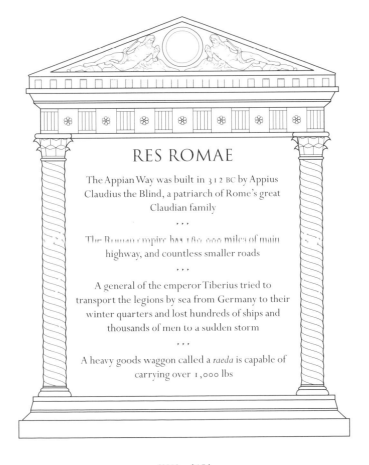

RES ROMAE

The Appian Way was built in 3 1 2 BC by Appius Claudius the Blind, a patriarch of Rome's great Claudian family

. . .

The Roman empire has 180,000 miles of main highway, and countless smaller roads

. . .

A general of the emperor Tiberius tried to transport the legions by sea from Germany to their winter quarters and lost hundreds of ships and thousands of men to a sudden storm

. . .

A heavy goods waggon called a *raeda* is capable of carrying over 1,000 lbs

give a few hints. Water, usually that most plentiful of products, is sold here. The bread is the best you can get anywhere, so the wise traveller will pack a few extra loaves for the journey ahead. . . .

Beneventum now, and the mountains of Apulia, which I know so well [Horace was born in Venusia, not far from here]. There was a burning wind scorching through the mountains and we would have failed to stagger through them had we not found lodgings at an inn near Trivicum. The inn itself was filled with eye-stinging smoke, because damp branches, leaves and all, had been thrown into the fire. Like an idiot, I spent half the night waiting for a deceitful girl. When I finally fell asleep, I had an erotic dream – and wet the bedclothes.

At Caudium an over-enthusiastic innkeeper almost burned his establishment to the ground while roasting some scrawny thrushes on a spit. The fire spat sparks onto the floor, and the flames raced through that ancient kitchen and went roaring up toward the roof. What a sight! Hungry guests and terrified slaves grabbing at the food and everyone else trying to fight the fire.

NAME THAT ROAD

actus – branch road, often used by livestock

clivus – street on a slope

pervium – thoroughfare

semita – lane

angiportus – narrow street or alley

via – road

vicus – street

Varius and Vergil [another famous poet] met us at Sinuessa. . . . We spent the night in a little house near the Campanian bridge.

Forum Apii on the way to Aricia is full of boatmen and grasping innkeepers. Being lazy, we spread this part of the trip over two days, though an energetic traveller can make it in one. But the Appian Way is less of a strain if you take it easy. The water at Forum Apii is unbelievably vile, so I went hungry while my fellow travellers had their dinner. And as night spread shadows over the earth and sprinkled stars in the sky, the slaves were jeering at the boatmen, and the boatmen bantered with the slaves. The blasted mosquitoes and the frogs croaking in the marsh made sleep impossible. Meanwhile, a boatman and a passenger, both sozzled on cheap wine, took turns serenading their absent girlfriends.

HORACE, *SATIRES* 5

The marsh Horace mentions is part of the Pomptine marshes, a famous haunt of bandits. But after that point the villas are closer together, and their furnishings more ornate. Not farms, but market gardens line the roadside, and the traffic is denser, more bustling. A few leagues more, and Rome awaits!

THE ENVIRONS
OF ROME

Villas · Aqueducts · Tombs
The Pomerium · Walls & Gates

II

VEN AS THE SMOKE FROM ROME'S half a million or so hearth fires, forges and bakeries becomes visible as a smudge on the horizon, the world's largest city imposes itself on the local landscape. From the grand villas on hillsides to the endless miles of market gardens and the huge stone aqueducts marching across the landscape, the countryside round about has been pressed into the service of this great city. From here, Rome makes itself ever more strongly felt as the first tombs appear on family plots on the sides of the road, up to when you reach the city walls and cross the *pomerium*, the sacred boundary of Rome itself.

VILLAS

NEAR ROME, COUNTRY BUILDINGS begin to look remarkably unrustic. Some roads leading off the Appian Way are marked by particularly grand gateways leading to the imposing villas that command the best views on nearby slopes and hillsides. Before, most of the villas along the road were working farm buildings (*villae rusticae*); now there are suburban villas with grander edifices (the *pars urbana*)

where wealthy owners reside when visiting from the city. The function of these villas is less agricultural than to provide Rome's elite with refuge from the heat, noise and distractions of city life.

There is no sudden change from farms to suburban villas, though the latter increasingly predominate as you approach Rome. Even the most elegant retreats generally do a bit of farming on the side, if only to give the owner his personal supply of fruit and vegetables. If conditions are suitable, many landowners dabble in viticulture; excellent quality wine gives the owner boasting rights, and even poor wine can be used for vinegar and antiseptic. Likewise the ponds in those delicately manicured gardens often have the practical purpose of supplying fish for the table. We hear of one Vedius Pollio, who kept lampreys:

When one of his slaves had broken a crystal cup, Vedius ordered him to be thrown to the huge lampreys which he had in his fish pond. ...The boy slipped from the captors' hands and fled to [Augustus] Caesar's feet asking nothing else other than a different way to die – he did not want to be eaten. Caesar was moved by the nov-

elty of the cruelty and ordered him to be released, all the crystal cups to be broken before his eyes, and the fish pond to be filled in.

SENECA, *ON ANGER* 3.40

Not all masters were as brutal as Pollio. The senator Pliny wrote to a friend saying that his villa was so designed that he had rooms to which he could withdraw 'so I do not disturb my slaves when they are relaxing nor do they disturb me at my work'. In this letter Pliny lovingly describes his retreat, which was by the sea some 17 miles from Rome. He describes a wide D-shaped lawn, surrounded by plane trees with ivy-covered trunks. There are cypresses around the outer circuit to provide dense shadow, while the raised pathways nearer the lawn are open to the sun.

Pliny carefully describes his villa as elegant and cultured, because one of the main functions of a suburban villa is to demonstrate what an elegant and cultured owner it has. Many of those villas on the way to Rome are veritable treasure houses of fine art, imported (or looted) from across the length and breadth of Rome's empire.

Almost everyone who can afford it has a peristyle; that is, a line of columns enclosing the interior of the building itself. Like most Roman private houses, villas look inward, being built around a central courtyard with gardens, and often a pond in the middle area. Because many villas also function as working farm buildings, there may be a second courtyard (the *pars rustica*) built for handling livestock, with rooms for storing and maintaining agricultural implements. With such villas, the owner will proudly show visitors both parts, sophisticated and rustic, for the Romans treasure their rural heritage:

What joy, amidst such feasts, to see the sheep,
Full of the pasture, hurrying homewards come;
To see the wearied oxen, as they creep,
Dragging the upturned ploughshare slowly home!

HORACE, *EPODE* 2

Those journeying towards Rome past Tibur (later called Tivoli) should beg, bribe or trade favours to get among the spectacular gardens and statues of the emperor Hadrian's villa. This massive complex is itself the size of a small town. It has lakes, fountains, libraries, baths, temples and a theatre. Some parts, such as the Canopus pool, have an Egyptian theme – a sad reminder of the emperor's lost love, a youth called Antinoos, who drowned in the Nile.

Those coming to Rome from the north will pass the villa at Prima Porta which

At the upper end is a semicircular bench of white marble, shaded with a vine which is trained to grow over four small pillars of Carystian marble. Water gushes ... into a stone cistern underneath. When I eat here, the tray of appetizers and the larger dishes are placed round the edge, while the smaller ones swim about in the form of little ships and waterbirds

PLINY, *LETTERS* 5 2

belonged to Livia, wife of the emperor Augustus, and can see there the splendid statue of the emperor dressed in armour with his *paludamentum* (general's cloak) wrapped around his waist.

AQUEDUCTS

NOTHING WILL PREPARE ONE FOR THE grandeur of the city of Rome more than its aqueducts. Even 40 miles from the city they march along the horizon for mile after mile. Massive as the aqueducts appear to be, they represent only a fraction of the 250-mile water supply network of the city. This runs through mountains and over

Such a variety of structures, carrying water from so many places. Compare this, please, with the pointless pyramids, or the useless (though decorative) constructions of the Greeks! ... The water commissioners are to take great care to ensure that the public fountains deliver water as continuously as possible, so that people may use them day and night

FRONTINUS, *AQUEDUCTS* 16 & 103

ROME'S MAIN AQUEDUCTS

Aqua Alsietina	Constructed by Augustus, it had the lowest level of all. A poor water supply; not unexpectedly, the main clients were in Transtiberim.
Aqua Appia	The oldest of the aqueducts, built in 312 BC by Appius Claudius the Blind.
Aqua Claudia	Started by Caligula in AD 38 and finished by Claudius. Has almost the same source as the Aqua Marcia.
Aqua Julia	Built by Agrippa in 33 BC, this was a productive aqueduct, supplying over 50,000 cubic metres a day.
Aqua Marcia	Built in 144 BC by Quintus Marcius Rex, this aqueduct at one time supplied the Capitol and the Quirinal.
Aqua Tepula	Built 125 BC. Runs underground for much of its course. Like the Aqua Marcia, this aqueduct drew its supply from the same springs that furnish much of the water supply of Rome 2,000 years later.
Aqua Traiana	Built by Trajan, and draws its supply from a local lake, the Lacus Sabatinus (21st-century Lake Bracciano).
Aqua Virgo	Lowest of all the aqueducts except Appia and Alsietina, it delivered one of the highest flows of water to the city – over 100,000 cubic metres a day.

rivers, and is so solidly built that it is perhaps the world's only municipal service that will still be partly functional after 1,800 years of use.

Each aqueduct begins and ends with a reservoir. Those at the beginning regulate the flow of water into the aqueduct and are deep and still, allowing any sediment carried into the reservoir to settle. Within the aqueduct, the water runs over a bed waterproofed with concrete, its flow regulated by large valve-like calixes made from bronze. The reservoirs at the

All the abundant supply of water ... for public buildings, baths and gardens ... coming from such a distance, tunnelling through mountains, and levelling the route through deep valleys must make this the most remarkable achievement anywhere in the world

PLINY, *NATURAL HISTORY* 36.121.2

end of the journey store the water for release into the pipes that deliver it to almost every street corner in Rome.

Not all Roman aqueducts are equal. Perhaps the best water comes from the Aqua Marcia, which is supplied from springs rising in the hills far from Rome. Another source of sparkling fresh water is appositely named the Maiden (the Aqua Virgo), after the young lady who pointed the springs out to soldiers searching for a fresh supply.

Though the system has multiple redun-

The Aqua Claudia and the older Aqua Marcia sweep across the countryside towards Rome. The Aqua Marcia alone cost 180 million sesterces – a truly monumental sum.

dancies built in to allow different aqueducts to serve different parts of Rome in need, some of the earlier aqueducts have starting points too low to serve the higher parts of Rome. Visitors should check which aqueducts serve the region where they will be staying, since a break in supply, or even a particularly dry summer, might leave them dependent on the truly vile water of the Alsietinian aqueduct, which usually serves industry (such as fullers) and waters gardens. Also try to avoid areas served by the Aqua Anio, though recent improvements have made its waters more potable than even when the aqueduct was new. Remember also that a long stay in Rome involves a degree of poisoning by the lead from which most pipes are made. The Romans know this, but believe that the public health gain from a ready supply of fresh water outweighs the cost.

The watering of gardens is a constant source of friction between the Roman upper class and the authorities. The public water supply is free, and a certain percentage of the rest is earmarked for those who have paid a special tax to receive it. However, some enterprising individuals tap the aqueducts on their way into Rome, or siphon off a clandestine supply from the municipal water pipes. Many city water commissioners start by ostentatiously destroying illegal pipes, and then build a retirement nest-egg from payments to look the other way as the pipes are restored.

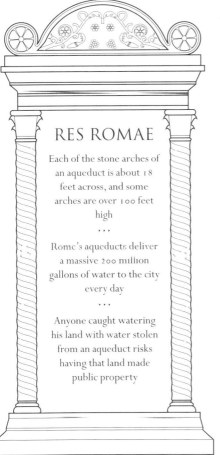

RES ROMAE

Each of the stone arches of an aqueduct is about 18 feet across, and some arches are over 100 feet high

· · ·

Rome's aqueducts deliver a massive 200 million gallons of water to the city every day

· · ·

Anyone caught watering his land with water stolen from an aqueduct risks having that land made public property

TOMBS

I T IS ILLEGAL TO BURY CORPSES WITHIN the sacred city of Rome itself, though the privilege may be granted to an extremely distinguished individual. Only Rome's great Valerian family, Vestal Virgins and the Caesars themselves have this as a right, and the Valerians choose not to exercise it. The Romans, hardened to massive child mortality, might bury the very young in the garden, as we might inter a deceased pet. Everyone else is buried outside the city, so the approach to Rome is lined with an increasing number of tombs, from the extremely modest to monumentally massive. There is no consensus on what a tomb should look like, so there is considerable variety in ornamentation and shape. The

Lie lightly on her, earth, for she was never heavy on you

MARTIAL, *EPITAPH TO A SLAVE CHILD*

early Romans buried their dead, but for centuries cremation has been the norm, though still not universally adopted – and recently burial has come into fashion. Among the graves, tombs and tombstones containing the bones or ashes of the departed are random edifices like little dovecotes (*columbaria*) with the serried urns of the cremated tucked within.

Amid the dead, the occasional family is seated at a picnic, as the Romans quite enjoy taking a meal with the dear departed. A funeral meal at the time of interment is followed by a second meal, the *cena novendialis*, at the burial site nine days later, and this may be repeated at least annually during festivals such as the Parentalia. Indeed the deceased is often taken to his resting place propped up on pillows, reclining as though about to enjoy a meal, as in the relief opposite. Cremations take place on a funeral pyre, or *rogus,* in a particular corner of each cemetery, with the potential for friction when the wind is blowing in the direction of a funeral dinner.

Most Romans belong to funeral clubs which take a small payment every month towards the cost of the contributor's funeral. One coin is returned by being placed in the mouth of the deceased as the fare for Charon, the ferryman who takes their spirit across the river Styx to the underworld. Some are buried with boots for the journey, or lamps to light their way underground.

RES ROMAE

The name 'sarcophagus' comes from the limestone of which the coffins are made. The chemicals in the stone can dissolve a body within weeks. (*Sarco* means 'flesh', and *phagus* 'eater'.)

Roman funeral procession. The corpse is taken for cremation dressed in his best toga and reclining on a couch as though at a banquet – a very public reminder to the city of what a distinguished son it has lost.

The Romans conscientiously assist future demographers by recording the age of the deceased on tombstones generally along with the letters DM (*Dis Manibus*, 'to the spirits of the underworld'; roughly the equivalent of RIP). Inscriptions may carry details of the grieving parent or spouse who erected the memorial (or sometimes slaves may erect a monument to their late master, thus fulfilling one of the conditions by which they were freed in his will). Sometimes the elegies are unexpectedly moving, such as this:

Stop for a moment, stranger, and read this brief message. This ugly tomb houses a lovely woman, called Claudia by her parents. She loved her husband wholeheartedly and gave him two sons. One is still on this earth, the other is under it. She was a lively companion, yet demure. She kept house and spun wool. That's all. Now be on your way.

Typically, such inscriptions are on a sarcophagus, a large stone coffin. A family tomb, such as that of the Scipios which is in a small side street off the Appian Way, may contain many of these.

Among the tombs on the way to Rome is the 36-foot-high tomb of Caecilia Metella, daughter-in-law to Licinius Crassus, the man who defeated the rebel gladiator Spartacus. Decorated with a distinctive frieze of ox skulls, the tomb rests on a square base well over 96 feet across, though the structure itself is round, as are the tombs (within Rome) of Augustus and Hadrian. While on the Appian Way, look out also for the *columbaria* of the imperial cooks and the sailors from the fleet at Misenum who lifted the massive sunshades over the Colosseum arena. At the ninth milestone the tombs are joined by the last of the *mutationes*, the little stables where imperial messengers change horses. From here, it is a straight run into Rome itself.

THE POMERIUM

FOR A ROMAN GENERAL, OR A PROVIN-
cial governor, the journey to the city
comes to an end at the *pomerium*, the city
limits of Rome, for these officials are forbidden to cross into Rome itself. The same
ancient stricture also applies to royalty,
and even the famous Cleopatra was
banned from central Rome when she came
to visit her lover, Julius Caesar.

The *pomerium* is demarcated by neatly
spaced white stones called *cippi*. For over a
thousand miles everything outside the line
belongs to Rome, everything within is the
city that the land outside belongs to. The
cippi mark the line of the plough, originally
guided by Romulus, which was drawn to
mark the city boundaries. Following
ancient Etruscan ritual, the plough was
carefully lifted over those stretches of
ground designated for the city's gates. The
pomerium has been enlarged since, but care
has been taken to keep some parts of the
city outside. Even the senate meets beyond
the *pomerium* on occasion so that senators
with duties that do not allow them within
can still attend. Likewise, the temple of
Bellona, Rome's goddess of war, is outside
the *pomerium* for those serving generals
who need an urgent word with the lady.
Many gods who are not part of Rome's
official pantheon also have their temples
parked on the city's official limits.

Even before crossing the *pomerium* you
may come across a reminder of how different and casually brutal Roman society can
be. Those cries you hear come from babies
screaming from hunger or thirst. Others
simply lie, too weak even to whimper.
These newborns have been left by their
parents as *res vacantes* (things of which the
owner has abandoned possession) either to
die or to be picked up by anyone who feels
like it. Some are deformed, some are
female, born into households that cannot
support another girl. The luckiest will be
taken into families that want them (this is a
common theme in Roman storytelling).
Others may be taken for household slaves
or pets (*delicia*), and some of the girls for
brothels. Even the ungentle Romans are
shamed and distressed by the practice, and
later emperors have launched funds to
subsidize children who would otherwise
be left in this way. Abandoned children can
be found anywhere in Rome, but particularly at the Columna Lactaria in the
vegetable market (Forum Holitorium).

WALLS & GATES

WITH THE FRONTIERS FAR FROM ROME,
the capital city may seem to have
little need of walls, yet controlling access
makes maintaining the gates worthwhile,
and the thought of rebel armies makes
emperors look after the ancient fortifications, and even extend them on occasion.
The original walls of Rome are tufa, a clay
that hardens to rock-like solidity on exposure to air. It is so tough that one part will
outlast emperors and medieval popes to
stand outside the railway station of the
later city.

Because the city has expanded, large
portions lie outside the wall. The wall
itself begins at the Tiber, runs over the low

ground to the south-west of the Capitoline hill, and then north-eastward where its defensive potential is supplemented by the natural cragginess of the terrain. It follows the Quirinal hill (see the **Seven Hills** pp. 25–30) and then dives into the valley between the Quirinal and the Pincian hills. Then it bears south across the flatter portions of the Esquiline hill, and dips to guard the valley between Esquiline and Caelian hills. From there it girds the south-west slopes of the Aventine hill, and passes to the south of the old cattle market before joining the Tiber to complete its seven-mile circuit.

As the Caelian hill looms ever higher over the approach from the Appian Way, a shady grove called the Camenae, sacred to

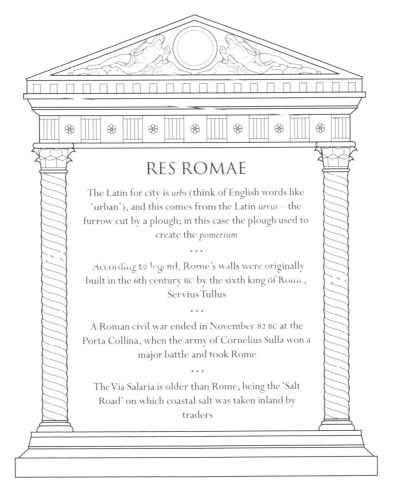

RES ROMAE

The Latin for city is *urbs* (think of English words like 'urban'), and this comes from the Latin *urvus* – the furrow cut by a plough; in this case the plough used to create the *pomerium*

, , ,

According to legend, Rome's walls were originally built in the 6th century BC by the sixth king of Rome, Servius Tullus

, , ,

A Roman civil war ended in November 82 BC at the Porta Collina, when the army of Cornelius Sulla won a major battle and took Rome

, , ,

The Via Salaria is older than Rome, being the 'Salt Road' on which coastal salt was taken inland by traders

the Muses, leads to the Porta Capena, which is one of the 15 major gates that pierce the city wall. Through this gate passed the legions which won Rome its empire, and by entering through this gate many a general gave up his command, even as he celebrated his victories with a Roman triumph. Observe the dimensions of the gate, for it is probably here that Pompey, the great general and rival of Julius Caesar, was mightily embarrassed.

[In 211 BC] Hannibal rode up to the Porta Collina with 2,000 cavalry, as far as the temple of Hercules, surveying the walls and the layout of the city from the best viewpoint he could get

LIVY, *HISTORY OF ROME* 36.10.3

He [Pompey]... intended to have the chariot at his triumph drawn with four elephants (having brought over several which belonged to the African kings), but on approaching the gates of the city he found them too tight a fit, and was forced to abandon his intention.

The Porta Capena pierces the walls alongside the massive arches of the Aqua Marcia, which enters at the same point. Those arriving from the east will have travelled down the Via Salaria and entered through the Porta Collina, the hill gate.

Those bound for the prosperous suburb between the Campus Martius and the Capitoline may opt to skirt the walls and enter by the Porta Flumentana (the river gate).

All the gates are rich in Roman legend. At the south-west of the Capitoline is the Porta Carmentalis, through which Rome's great Fabian clan marched to war and disaster against the Etruscans in 306 BC, while the Porta Raudusculana sports a pair of bronze horns to honour Genucius Cipus. As his army marched out through that gate the general was told in a prophecy that he would overthrow the Roman Republic when he returned. To avoid this, Cipus remained in exile until he died.

SETTLING IN

Where to Stay — the Seven Hills
Types of Accommodation · Sanitary Facilities
Medical Emergencies · What to Wear · Food

III

WHERE TO STAY –
THE SEVEN HILLS

ON ARRIVAL IN ROME, TAKE STOCK FOR a few moments. Where you are going to stay should not just be determined by the cost of your lodgings. The type of housing, quality of neighbour, distance to the sanitary facilities, and how far you are prepared to walk to anywhere interesting or important are all vital considerations. When meeting Romans, knowing the basics of what to wear and what to eat will help to avoid unnecessary social embarrassment. Nothing is guaranteed to ruin a good dinner party like a guest who turns up wrongly dressed, and then blanches (or worse) when confronted with sow's udders stuffed with giant African snails. And since Rome operates without street signs – on the friendly principle that if you don't know where you are, you probably don't belong and shouldn't be there – some basic grasp of city navigation is essential.

The seven heads are seven hills on which the woman sits. And the woman is that great city which reigns over the kings of the earth

REVELATIONS 17

The Romans navigate by their hills. You may hear phrases like 'Aulus lives on the Caelian,' or 'It's one of those shops in the Quirinal-Viminal valley,' so it is important to know which hills are where. Everyone knows that Rome has seven hills, but in fact the reality is more complicated. Let us start in the north and work around clockwise to meet each hill in turn.

THE QUIRINAL: HOME TO ROME'S UPPER middle class. Furthest north, at 12 o'clock on this imaginary dial, is the Quirinal hill, which faces south towards the Roman Forum with the old military training fields of the Campus Martius to the west. On the north side are the beautifully cultured Gardens of Sallust. The Quirinal is not really a separate hill but one of a series of projections from an ancient volcanic ridge running north-eastward across the side of the city. We will meet the other projections in due course. The Quirinal was originally settled by the Sabine people, and the Forum was at first the meeting place between the Sabines and the Romans who settled on the nearby Palatine. If so, the Sabines were there first, since archaeological evidence shows settlements on the Quirinal hill at least two centuries before Romulus founded his city.

Visitors will almost certainly spend some time on the Quirinal, since it now houses Rome's finest shopping arcades. Before the general Vespasian became emperor, his family lived here, and you can still visit the *templum gentis Flaviae* (the temple of the Flavian family) which was built on the site of the ancestral home by Vespasian's son Domitian.

THE VIMINAL: CINDERELLA OF ROME'S hills. The next door neighbour of the Quirinal hill is the Viminal, a slightly smaller (and less fashionable) projection from the volcanic ridge. The Viminal is named after the osiers which grew there

---

THE REGIONES: ROME'S POSTCODES/ZIP CODES

Since the time of Augustus Rome has been divided into 14 *regiones* for administrative purposes. Most Romans refer to areas by the hills and valleys, and then get specific with particular neighbourhoods (*vici*). Nevertheless, knowing the location of the regions helps in dealing with 'officialdom'.

Region I The area between the Porta Capena (the gate the Appian Way goes out through) and the Caelian hill

Region II Essentially the Caelian hill itself

Region III The bottom of the Esquiline, including parts of Nero's old Golden House and the Colosseum

Region IV The Subura, i.e. the valley between the Esquiline and Viminal, and bits of the Velia including Vespasian's temple and forum

Region V The upper slopes of the Esquiline – the area behind Region III as you go out from the centre of town

Region VI Most of the Quirinal and parts of the Viminal that are not in Region IV

Region VII The eastern part of the Campus Martius and the Pincian hill

Region VIII The heart of Rome – the Capitoline and the Forum of the Romans

Region IX The south-west part of the Campus Martius, extending as far south as the Tiber island

Region X Imperial Rome – the Palatine

Region XI The cattle market, the Circus Maximus and the rest of the valley between the Palatine and Aventine

Region XII The mainly residential area to the south of Region XI

Region XIII The Aventine and its river frontage, including the Emporium adjoining the cattle market

Region XIV The largest area, also called Transtiberim, consisting of the Tiber island, but mostly the area on the west of the Tiber, home to much of Rome's immigrant population

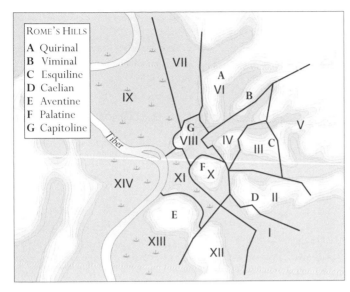

ROME'S HILLS

A Quirinal
B Viminal
C Esquiline
D Caelian
E Aventine
F Palatine
G Capitoline

Diagram of Rome's regions (I–XIV) and hills (A–G). Those looking for the best postal addresses should consider II and VI. The Subura district, IV, is not particularly salubrious and nor is XIV (Transtiberim). Try XII or XIII for a happy medium. VIII and X are reserved for gods and emperors.

(*vimina* in Latin). The hill contains few monuments or grand residences. Housing here tends to be cheaper than on the Quirinal, though the aristocracy maintain some fine residences scattered about on the hill (and almost everywhere else in Rome as well). Even most of the traffic passes on either side of the hill, though the Viminal gate leads to the barracks of Rome's elite Praetorian Guard.

THE ESQUILINE: KINGS AT THE TOP, slums at the bottom. At 3 o'clock on our imaginary dial is the largest of the projections from the ridge: the Esquiline hill. In fact the Esquiline is so large that it has several sub-divisions. The small ridge on the north-east slope is called the Cispius, the western side is the Fagutal, and the southern side is the Oppian. There is also a long ridge called the Velia which connects the Esquiline with the Palatine. If staying on the Esquiline, visitors need to check carefully where they are lodging. The best accommodation is on the upper slopes and from there things go downhill metaphorically as well as literally. The lower slopes are part of the notoriously rough and slum-like Subura district, and if the inhabitants do not kill you, the shoddy housing might have a go, being prone to fires in summer and spontaneous collapse in winter.

The hill did have some distinguished inhabitants. King Tullus Hostilius lived here while Rome was still ruled by kings, as did Valerius Poplicola, the Republican rebel who helped to end their rule. Nero built the vestibule of his splendid (though short-lived) palace at the foot of the Esquiline, on the Velia, close to where Hadrian's temple of Venus and Rome now stands.

THE CAELIAN: MILLIONAIRES WELCOME. The southernmost spur of the ridge is the Caelian hill, allegedly named after an Etruscan adventurer called Caelius Vibenna, who settled there. It has two peaks; the major Caelian, to the west, and the little Caelian to the north. As with all the hills of Rome, the wealthy prefer to live on the higher slopes, away from the noise, smoke and dirt of the valleys, but the occupants of the Caelian are wealthier than most. A temple to the memory of the emperor Claudius graces this hill, built by Claudius' last wife (and probable murderer) Agrippina. There is also a military presence: the *equites singulares*, the cavalry escort of the emperor, are based here.

THE AVENTINE: THE PEOPLE'S HILL. The Aventine, at 7 o'clock on the dial is the most southerly of the seven hills. The Tiber flows along its western side and to the north is the old cattle market, with the Palatine hill just to the east of that. The Aventine is particularly favoured by Rome's plebeians, who twice withdrew to its slopes, officially seceding from the rest of Rome because they were particularly displeased with its rulers. The Aventine was outside the *pomerium* until AD 49. Consequently one Roman eccentric chose to be buried at the bottom of the southern slope in a splendid white marble pyramid which shows every sign of lasting as long as its Egyptian predeces-

Should men like this ... who were brought to Rome with the prunes and figs ... be seated higher at dinner than we, who breathed our first on the Aventine?

JUVENAL (IN XENOPHOBIC MOOD), *SATIRES* 3.80

sors. Its position outside the *pomerium* also made the Aventine home to the temples of many 'foreign' deities. However, there are also temples to the native gods of Rome, and a very ancient temple to the goddess Ceres. For many years the Aventine was one of the most cosmopolitan areas of Rome, with many outsiders attracted by the fact that much of the hill was public land (*ager publicus*). Lately, the well-to-do merchant class have been moving in, attracted by the Aventine's panoramic views and the nearby docks. In fact so many *amphorae* (clay barrels) have been unloaded by trading ships that their fragments form a separate mountain on the river banks – the Mons Testaceus.

THE PALATINE: THE HILL THAT EMPERORS call 'home'. Even when Rome was a republic, the address which really counted was the one on the centre of our dial – the oldest hill of Rome, the Palatine. One of the must-see sites of Rome is Romulus' thatched hut on the south-west corner of the Palatine. Although others swear that Romulus' hut was on the Capitoline, the Palatine faction have a hut to show. True, the thatch was replaced once or twice, the occasional wall collapsed in a fire, and the roof beams were changed when they rotted through, but it's the exact house Romulus lived in, honestly. The Palatine is 25 acres of the most opulent buildings that money can buy, a flat-topped hill with two separate peaks – the Palatium and the Ceramulus. An orator called Hortensius had a house on the north-west side which was later occupied by the emperor Augustus. Like the house of Romulus, reverent later generations have kept the house as its great occupant left it. So far have the times changed that a later writer commented on most of the furnishings being so crude that people would not accept them even as gifts in his day.

Augustus turned the Palatine into Rome's seat of government, so passing the word 'palace' to later generations. Apart from the buildings occupied by the imperial family and its servants and bodyguards, most of the hill is given over to administration. There is also a temple to Apollo at the top (founded by Augustus) and a temple to Jupiter Stator at the base (allegedly founded by Romulus). Much of the building on the site today, including a splendid hippodrome at the top, is the work of the emperor Domitian and his architect Rabirius.

Romulus opened the Asylum on the spot where, as you go down from the Capitol, you find an enclosed space between two groves

LIVY, *HISTORY OF ROME* 1.8

THE CAPITOLINE: ROME'S TEMPLE AND fortress. From the Palatine we move in an 11 o'clock direction towards the southwards bend of the Tiber and the double-peaked hill of Rome's most ancient fortress – the Capitoline. The Romans generally call the whole hill the Capitoline, though this properly should refer to the southern peak only. The other peak is called the Arx. In the saddle between the two stands an ancient temple to the divine Asylaeus, where the original Romans gave shelter to any who sought sanctuary within. Like the palace (Palatine) and the capitol (Capitoline), this temple – the 'asylum' – has become a part of everyday language.

For the Romans, the very centre of Rome, Rome's empire, and all that Rome stands for is the temple of Jupiter Capitolinus Optimus Maximus – Jupiter of the Capitoline Hill: the Best and Greatest.

This temple stands on the foundations built by the Tarquins in the last days of the monarchy. Burned down in the last turbulent days of the Republic, rebuilt and destroyed again in the civil wars of AD 69, the temple in its current form is the work of the emperor Domitian. At the Arx you will find the temple of Juno, the consort of Jupiter, and also the *auguraculum*, where the city's priests came to observe signs from the heavens such as the flight of birds or shooting stars. And, talking of things falling to earth, on the Capitoline overlooking the Forum is the notorious Tarpeian rock. Here criminals and traitors are thrown to their doom, following the Roman principle that justice should not only be done, but seen to be done as messily and spectacularly as possible.

The Capitoline hill is even less residential than the Palatine. As well as being the religious and defensive core of Rome, the hill holds the massive Tabularium, the Record Office of the Roman state, where amongst other records are the minutes of senate meetings.

Though not among the traditional seven hills of Rome, three other hills are very significant to the life of the city. The Pincian hill, where the super-rich live amid such spectacular estates that the hill is sometimes known as the Garden hill; the Janiculum, a ridge that the Romans once regarded as their northern defensive boundary; and the Vatican hill. Romans know the Vatican hill principally for the nearby Circus of Nero, and regard with suspicion pilgrims to the tomb of the man they call St Peter.

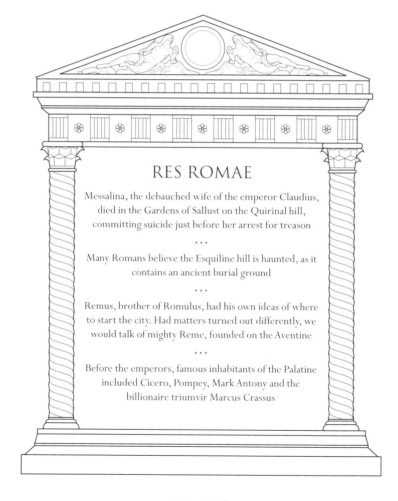

RES ROMAE

Messalina, the debauched wife of the emperor Claudius, died in the Gardens of Sallust on the Quirinal hill, committing suicide just before her arrest for treason

, , ,

Many Romans believe the Esquiline hill is haunted, as it contains an ancient burial ground

, , ,

Remus, brother of Romulus, had his own ideas of where to start the city. Had matters turned out differently, we would talk of mighty Reme, founded on the Aventine

, , ,

Before the emperors, famous inhabitants of the Palatine included Cicero, Pompey, Mark Antony and the billionaire triumvir Marcus Crassus

Followers of the cult of Chrestus (as he is known in these times) will probably seek lodgings among the Levantine and Jewish traders in the Transtiberim district just outside the *pomerium* to the west of the Tiber, one of the most cosmopolitan areas in a thoroughly cosmopolitan city.

TYPES OF ACCOMMODATION

FOR RENT AS FROM JULY 1

SHOPS WITH STREET FRONTAGE AND COUNTER SPACE

LUXURIOUS SECOND-STOREY APARTMENTS AND ONE TOWN HOUSE

ANYONE INTERESTED, SORT THINGS OUT WITH PRIMUS, SLAVE OF GNAEUS ALLIUS NIGIDUS MAIUS

WHERE YOU STAY IN ROME DEPENDS upon your budget, your needs, and how long you intend to remain in town. Most of the living quarters in Rome are rented, and most landlords will be happy to rent rooms by the month, the week, or even (for requirements of a particular nature) by the hour (see **Entertainment** p. 80). Advertisements, like this one above right from Pompeii, can be seen painted on the walls of vacant tenancies.

However, rather than renting, visitors would ideally stay with a *hospes*, a friend who has offered hospitality in a town house, preferably on one of the better hills, high enough to catch the breeze, but not so high as to be out of reach of the aqueducts.

On busy streets such houses often have cubicles built into the front where small shops offer a variety of clothing, artifacts or snacks. In quieter areas, the walls are often painted red for the first four or five feet and white thereafter. The windowless, fortress-like façade is unbroken except for a very solid wooden door which, even if open, will have a custodian on sentry duty just within – a reminder that Rome by night can be a very lawless place. 'You'll be

considered a pretty careless type if you go out for dinner without making a will,' remarks the satirist Juvenal. 'Be grateful if nothing worse than a bucketful of slops hits you over the head on the way home. This town is full of violent drunks who can't sleep well until they have beaten someone up.' Roman readers can sympathize with Apuleius in his novel *The Golden Ass*, which, though not set in Rome, gives this reminder of why strong doors are important.

And when I came into the first street my torch went out ... I could hardly find my way home, stumbling along in the dark. And when I was just about at the door, I saw three extraordinarily burly individuals struggling with the gate to get in. When they saw me, they paid no attention, but tried yet harder to break down the doors. Reasonably enough, I concluded that these were thieves of the most brazen kind, so taking the sword I carried under my cloak for just that reason, I drew and had at them ....

APULEIUS, *THE GOLDEN ASS* 11

Roman apartment blocks. Most of the population live in houses such as these, with handy shops and restaurants at the bottom, and the better lodgings on the first floor. The walls of the lower floors are up to 6 feet thick as they support the rest of the building. This makes them well insulated against sound and changes in temperature.

Within the house, the first room is the *vestibulum*. This is generally a long, narrow hallway for parking street clothes and boots, but in the houses of more important Romans, this is a semi-public space where clients gather in the morning to pay their respects and ask for favours. The flickering light of the oil lamps may reveal a welcoming message in the mosaic on the floor such as *Salve* ('Greetings'), or that old favourite *Cave canem* ('Beware of the dog'). Beyond the *vestibulum* it can be seen that, like their country cousins, urban town houses are built around an atrium, with a space open to the sky, letting smoke from cooking fires out, and rainwater in to supplement the domestic water supply.

Around the side of the atrium are *cubic-*

> *What is holier and more strongly fortified by all religious awe than the house of each and every citizen?*
>
> CICERO, *ON HIS HOUSE* 109

ula, small rooms used for relaxing, reading or sleeping. Even in rather grand houses, *cubicula* are very definitely cubicle-sized. This is because a Roman's life is lived in public, either in the bosom of his (often extremely extensive) family, or with friends and associates. In a city where even bowel movements may take place in a social setting (see **Sanitary Facilities** p. 34) don't expect much private space for sleeping. Most Roman houses teem with life, from children racing about the columns of the atrium to toothless grandmothers sitting by the fire, slaves hurrying about their business, and second cousins, in-laws and other female relatives settling down to weaving or needlework accompanied by banter, gossiping or back-biting (domestic relationships among extended families can be fraught, and it is the job of the senior woman of the household, the *materfamilias*, to make sure all runs smoothly).

This is a good moment to introduce another of the problems of living in Rome – noise.

There is nowhere in this city where a poor man can have a quiet moment to gather his wits. Schoolteachers are deadly, first thing in the morning [Roman classes begin at dawn, and are

Even Boreas [the personification of the north wind] would find my flat draughty

MARTIAL, *EPIGRAMS* 8.14

. . .

Here in my attic I sleep with the pigeons, chilled by the rain sifting through the rafters, and the last to know that the building is on fire

JUVENAL, *SATIRES* 3,200–2

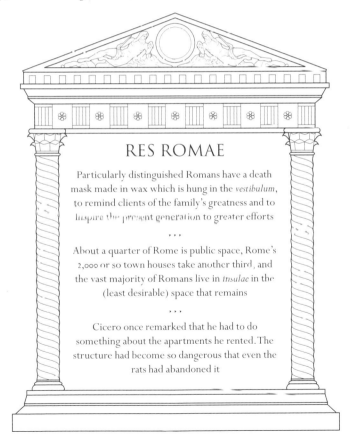

RES ROMAE

Particularly distinguished Romans have a death mask made in wax which is hung in the *vestibulum*, to remind clients of the family's greatness and to inspire the present generation to greater efforts

. . .

About a quarter of Rome is public space, Rome's 2,000 or so town houses take another third, and the vast majority of Romans live in *insulae* in the (least desirable) space that remains

. . .

Cicero once remarked that he had to do something about the apartments he rented. The structure had become so dangerous that even the rats had abandoned it

often held outdoors] and even before dawn the bakers will have wakened you. The coppersmiths hammering away jar your nerves all day, while here the money changer idly jangles coins on his grimy table, and there, a man hammering Spanish gold into dust whacks away at his worn-out stone with a shiny mallet.

MARTIAL, *EPIGRAMS* 12.57

... and at night ...

Well, here in Rome, sick people die from lack of sleep. ... Carts creak through the narrow, winding alleys, and the curses of their drivers would keep even a deaf man awake.

JUVENAL, *SATIRES* 3.232; 236–8

Partly for this reason, some town houses have relatively narrow frontages and extend back quite a distance from the street, with the garden at the far end.

Town houses in Rome are much less numerous than the huge apartment buildings, crammed six to eight together into blocks called *insulae*. These crowd the valleys and lower slopes of the hills, varying in quality from draughty bedsits to well-appointed multiroom apartments.

He spends all day on the toilet ... he's not sick, he's looking for a dinner invitation

MARTIAL, *EPIGRAMS* 11.77

The ideal apartment is on the first floor, secure from thieves, but easy to bring water and goods to. It is also low enough for the occupants to jump to safety in the event of a fire or a partial collapse.

An edict of Trajan keeps the height of apartment blocks to under 58 feet (usually five storeys), and Nero introduced fire regulations, but the one rule to remember is never to rent before a careful inspection.

SANITARY FACILITIES

THE ROMANS HAVE A HABIT OF SITING cesspits uncomfortably close to wells, so it will come as a relief to know that Rome itself has an extensive sewer system which is regularly flushed with waste water from the aqueducts. The oldest and largest of Rome's sewers is the Cloaca Maxima, which runs under the Forum and is large enough to take a boat through, if that is your idea of fun. Many apartment buildings have gravity-feed facilities connected to the sewers or to a central cesspit, but many others make use of the tried and trusted chamber pot. Sometimes ordure is collected for agricultural purposes; in other places it is simply dumped in the streets, which is why some streets have little stepping stones to allow members of the public to cross without soiling their feet.

Fullers, ever appreciative of uric acid for their trade, have placed large *amphorae* on street corners to receive the offerings of the public, who are still darkly outraged that the emperor Vespasian placed a twopenny charge on their use (which is why until the late 20th century, similar facilities in modern Paris were called *Vespasiannes*). Incidentally, when Vespasian was aedile – an official whose duties included keeping the streets clean – he was so bad at his job that the emperor Caligula ordered Vespasian's toga to be stuffed with the mess from the road.

Try to find lodgings close to a public bath, where a constant stream of waste water from the baths runs under the toilet seat, which is basically a bench with strategically situated holes on which you can sit and exchange the gossip of the day with fellow patrons of the facility. Watch for youths whose idea of a joke is to surreptitiously ignite a hank of wool soaked in oil in an upstream toilet. Having this burning mass sail just under your posterior can effectively ruin your day.

MEDICAL EMERGENCIES

THOSE WHO KNOW LITTLE OF MEDICINE in Rome, or in the ancient world as a whole, are advised to treasure their ignorance of things like Roman catheters and obstetric instruments. The best advice for those falling unexpectedly sick in Rome is – don't.

Rome is pretty much subject to the entire gamut of illnesses and infections. Though syphilis and bubonic plague do not seem to be numbered there, tuberculosis, leprosy and tetanus more than make up for their absence. Consider the advice of the respected physician Aretaeus to doctors treating a case of tetanus: 'It is one of those cases where it actually is forgiveable to pray to the gods that they take a man's life. You cannot save the patient, you cannot ease his pain, you cannot even straighten his limbs without severing or breaking them.'

Surgical instruments.

This is a world without antibiotics, where a casual graze can lead to blood poisoning and death through septicemia, and acute appendicitis is generally fatal. Looking at the array of ailments, one might wonder how any Roman survives for long, and the answer is that many don't. But remember that any adult Roman became so through an extremely robust immune system. The infant mortality rate is horrific. Since a Roman needs to be over 40 years old to become a senator, and the average life expectancy at birth is less than 30, any mature Roman is by definition a survivor.

While the Romans are almost powerless to treat disease, they have some solid ideas of how to avoid getting it. They know that it is best to avoid swamps, and Lucretius, a philosopher, gives this definition of germs. 'Tiny creatures, too small to see, that float through the air and enter the body through the mouth and nose. ... This can give rise to serious diseases.'

The Romans appreciate the importance of clean water, good diet and healthy exercise. 'Excellent health comes from taking good care of yourself', claims Galen, a famous and influential medical writer. In fact, anyone falling sick would do well to query if the attending physician is a follower of Galen, since Galen generally follows the advice of Hippocrates – 'first do no harm.'

This is not true of all doctors. One inscription notes of the treatment for a deformed back that the doctor 'placed three very large stones ... along the hunchback's spine'. The man was crushed to death, but the inscription notes caustically that 'he died straighter than a ruler'. (*Greek Anthology* 9.120.)

Cato the Elder warned his son against doctors, calling them conspirators sworn to the eradication of the Roman race. However, Cato also maintained the best way to raise a robust child was to bathe him regularly in the urine of a man who lived on a nothing but cabbage. (The annoying Roman penchant for po-faced humour makes it hard to establish how serious Cato was being here.)

Many doctors mix their medication with prescriptions for prayers and the wearing of amulets. This advice should be followed on the same basis that it is often dispensed. It certainly cannot harm, and who knows? It may help.

More practically, remember that woad (the stuff that turns ancient British warriors blue) is a useful antiseptic – certainly better than the wine and vinegar that many Romans use. Burns and scalds are generally treated with grape tannin, and the gum from certain trees may be placed under a bandage to retard heavy bleeding. For infected insect bites, ulcerations and similar problems, the Romans do a very useful calamine lotion, and poppy juice is available as an analgesic. Sufferers from severe toothache might be offered poppy head skins to place over the infected area (remember to spit rather than swallow saliva while the poultice is in place – the system can only take so much opium).

'Almost every bite has a poison of some sort,' says Celsus, and anyone bitten generally has the bite swabbed down immediately with vinegar. Sadly rabies is endemic, and the only remedy the Romans have is immediate cauterization of a bitten area, followed by swift amputation if possible. As Celsus notes, once hydrophobia sets in, water can be forced into a patient, but nothing can stop the fatal spasms as the disease works its way into the nervous system.

WHAT TO WEAR

UNLESS ON A FORMAL VISIT, THERE IS no need to pack a toga, and only Roman citizens are entitled to wear one anyway. The toga is, in any case, stiflingly hot in summer and draughty in winter. It is also heavy, being of wool and three times the wearer's height (or about 16.5 feet) by 10 feet across. This forms a large semicircle, which is worn by putting the straight edge over the left shoulder and wrapping it around one's back. Then it goes under the right shoulder, and back over the left shoulder again. Because it has no fastenings, unless the left elbow is kept constantly bent, the whole thing comes unravelled.

Experienced toga wearers manage to

A TOGA TELLS A LOT ABOUT THE WEARER

Toga candida – the wearer is standing for election (i.e. he is a candidate)

Toga virilis (or *pura*) – the undyed, off-white toga of a citizen

Toga praetexta – worn by underage children and magistrates

Toga pulla – of dark wool worn by workmen or those in mourning

Toga picta – purple toga worn by conquering generals and emperors

Toga trabea – striped toga worn by priests

get a superb pleated effect with their folds, and take care to fold down the straight edge where it passes under the right arm, which makes a large and comfortable pocket called a *sinus*. (Which is why if someone wriggles right into something, he is said to have insinuated himself.) However, these show-offs often have their togas put on them by a specialist slave, called a *vestiplicus,* who might also arrange for an extra droop at the back to make a small hood so that the wearer can cover his head while sacrificing. (Performing sacrifices on particular occasions is one of the duties of state officials and heads of households.)

Every Roman male wears a toga on certain occasions. When he formally becomes a man, he dons the *toga virilis*. He gets married in a toga, and when he dies the toga is wrapped around him to become his funeral shroud. A woman in a toga (the *toga muliebris*), is a prostitute. Respectable ladies wear a *stola*.

The *stola* consists of a front and back part sewn together to make a sort of tube.

It is held together at the top by two brooches, thus creating separate holes for the head and arms. A wide belt called a *zona* goes just under the breasts, and gives the dress some shape, though this is often hidden again by a square-cut blanket-like shawl called a *palla*. Unlike the rigid hierarchy of men's togas, the colours of a woman's *stola* are limited only by her taste and the dyes available. Most dyes come from vegetables or minerals and are not fixed. Therefore dresses tend to be all of

Roman family dressed to impress, not in everyday tunics (note the lady's modestly covered feet).

one colour, though reds, greens, blues and black are all on offer. For those who must have a two-tone dress, one of the tones has to be a purple, blue or red tint. This is *murex*, a fixed dye extracted from a species of snail which is rare enough for the dye to be very expensive.

Lest it be assumed that women's clothes lacked variety, consider this lament:

The ladies' tailor, the jeweler, the woollen worker — they're all hanging round. And there are the dealers in flounces and underwear and veils, in violet dyes and yellow dyes, or muffs, or balsam-scented footwear. Then the lingerie people drop in, along with shoemakers and squatting cobblers and slipper and sandal merchants and dealers in mallow dyes; and the belt makers swarm around, and the girdle makers along with them. And now you may suppose you've paid them all off. Then up pop the weavers and lace men and cabinet-makers — in their hundreds — who plant themselves like jailers in the vestibulum and want you to settle up. So you march them in and square accounts. 'All paid off now, anyway,' you may think, when in troop the blokes who do the saffron dyeing.

PLAUTUS, *THE POT OF GOLD* 508–22

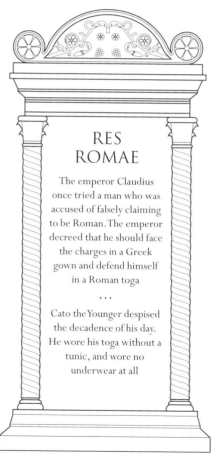

RES
ROMAE

The emperor Claudius once tried a man who was accused of falsely claiming to be Roman. The emperor decreed that he should face the charges in a Greek gown and defend himself in a Roman toga

* * *

Cato the Younger despised the decadence of his day. He wore his toga without a tunic, and wore no underwear at all

On less formal occasions, Romans of every age and social class wear tunics. These are basically knee-length T-shirts with a belt around the middle. Anything they want to carry is dropped down the neck of the tunic and held in place by the belt, which is why it is a common trick of Roman thieves to cut through someone's belt and grab whatever falls to the ground. A senator's tunic is distinguished by a broad stripe (the *latus clavus*) which he also has on his toga. Equestrians — the next rank down from senators — also have a stripe, but narrower.

Most people wear a *subligaculum*, literally 'a little something tied on underneath'. Despite the expense and sneers at one's decadence, it is well worth getting this garment in silk for the added comfort. For women, the same goes for the *mamillare*, a breast-band that serves as a proto-bra.

Ladies can wear whatever they like on their feet, as their *stola* should be long enough to hide them anyway. Seeing his inamorata's feet is enough to make a hot-blooded Roman male want to lie down (preferably with company). Generally, sandals are standard for men and women. When getting about town, sandals which enclose the entire foot are advisable (and should always be worn under the toga), but when indoors, remember to remove these and replace them with lighter thong sandals – no one wants the muck of the street tracked across their nice clean mosaics.

FOOD

You will dine nicely at my house, Julius Cerialis, if you have no better engagement, come. We will go to the baths together (you know how near Stephanus baths are to me) and there you can note when the eighth hour comes. [The Roman dinner cena *is eaten in the late afternoon, and the baths usually have sundials so patrons can keep track of the time.]*

First, you shall have lettuce ... and shoots cut from their parent leeks; then salted tuna, bigger than a small lizard-fish, and another garnished with eggs and leaves. There will be other eggs too, roasted in embers of moderate heat, a lump of cheese ripened in a Velabran street, and olives that have felt the Picenian frost. That's the appetizer: do you want to know the rest? I'll lie to make you come: fish, mussels, sows udder, and fat poultry and stuffed wild-fowl.

MARTIAL, *EPIGRAMS* 11.52

FOOD IS IMPORTANT TO THE ROMANS, and the taking of it generally a social occasion. Despite Martial's fantasies, meat is not an important part in the diet of most Romans, but vegetables and cheeses are plentiful. With growing prosperity, many Romans eat meat once a week or more, usually poultry, but also pork and beef. (Or both together in the 'Trojan pig' – a suckling pig stuffed with other meats.)

RES ROMAE

Foodstuffs you won't find in Rome include tomatoes, potatoes, peanuts, rice, cane sugar, chocolate, distilled liquor – and pasta

. . .

Some foods come a long way – spices from the Orient, and walnuts and special bread from Persia

. . .

Snails are a delicacy; special farms breed them in large numbers

Town houses usually have their own kitchens. There are different sized cauldrons for boiling things, while the ovens are beehive-shaped constructions of clay which are heated with wood or charcoal. When they have reached the appropriate temperature, the cinders are scraped out, and the food is placed within. Ovens are banned from most *insulae* on the reasonable grounds that the places are lethal enough fire-traps already. Most citizens take their regular state allocation of grain directly from miller to baker, and bring the food home as bread.

I've wined, I've dined,
I've concubined

PLAUTUS, *THE BROTHERS*
MENAECHMUS 476

The very poor can't afford to have their grain processed, and boiled wheat is their main diet. To supplement this, certain streets are designated for the food markets which move about the city on a regular basis, replacing the usual traffic with long rows of stalls selling clothing and farm produce (*see* **Shopping** p. 63). If you are after fresh fish, however, you would do better to go to one of the fixed markets, where the heavy stone tables have water-filled bowls carved into them and live fish swimming within. Bear in mind that the Mediterranean lacks the coastal shelves on which fish thrive, and so fish are relatively rare and correspondingly expensive.

Between the hills in the densely populated valleys of working-class Rome, it seems as though every second street-front shop is an eatery of some description. Some sell specialist snacks for one of Rome's many ethnic groups, others offer full-scale meals for the patrons relaxing under the awnings. Wine is freely available, as are delicacies like dates imported from Africa and Palmyra. Try for instance *dulcia domestica*, a delicious dessert of pitted dates stuffed with dried fruit, nuts, cake crumbs and spices, all soaked in fruit juice or wine.

The Romans like their food highly spiced, perhaps because, in a society with only rudimentary ideas of how to preserve food, a pungent taste disguises the fact that the food is past its best. Many dishes

GLIRES

Lean pork
Dormouse meat trimmings
(If you have no dormouse,
gerbil or hamster will do)
Ground black pepper
Mixed nuts
Several leaves of *laser* (rocket/arugula is
an acceptable substitute)
A soupçon of *liquamen*

Pound the mixture until it makes a rough paste suitable for forcing into your dormouse. Put the animal once stuffed in an earthen casserole dish. Boil in a pot with stock. Alternatively you can roast in the oven. (Take care not to let the ears burn!)

Roman cooking utensils.

include the piquant fish sauce *garum*, which is generally imported from Spain or the Middle East. To fully appreciate *garum*'s tangy flavour, note how the sauce is made. Fish guts and entire small fish such as sprats or anchovies are put into a large vat and salted. The whole mixture is left to ferment for a while, and then placed in a large shallow basin open to the sun (wine may be added to the mixture at this point). There it is left to 'mature' for a month or two, after which the putrefied mixture (*liquamen*) is strained through a tightly woven wooden basket. Boiled grape juice may be added before the mixture is packed into *amphorae* and shipped to Rome for your delectation.

Honey and fruit feature even in savoury dishes, giving Roman cookery a rather sweet-and-sour taste. The works of one Roman cookery writer Apicius have survived through the ages, and we finish this section with two descriptions, firstly one of Apicius' recipes (left – some parts have

been translated into 21st-century terms), and the next a luxurious meal prepared by the senator Pliny.

So, my fine fellow! You arrange to come to supper and then never appear.

Well, justice will be done – you will pay back every last denarius I splashed out on your account, and it's no small sum, let me tell you.

I had prepared, if you'd like to know, a lettuce apiece, three snails, two eggs, and a barley cake, with some sweet wine and snow (the snow I am most definitely going to charge you for, since it is now melted away over the salad). Olives, beetroot, gourds, onions, and a thousand other equally sumptuous delicacies were waiting for you ....

PLINY SECUNDUS TO SEPTITIUS CLARUS,
LETTERS 11

OUT AND ABOUT

Dining Out · Meeting People
Roman Names · The Social Order
Slaves · Family

IV

DINING OUT

ROME IS A CITY WITH A LARGE POPULA-tion of foreigners, and therefore a certain allowance for social ineptitude is made for strangers. That said, Roman society is stunningly snobbish and class conscious, so it is an excellent idea to keep the number of faux pas to a minimum.

> *If, when we meet, I'm cropped in awkward*
> *   style*
> *By some uneven barber, then you smile;*
> *You smile, if perhaps, my gown's askew,*
> *Or my overshirt is tatty while my tunic's new*
>
> HORACE, *EPISTLES* I.I

Forewarned is forearmed, so here are the basic armaments for understanding Roman society and culture, and particularly for action in the front line of Roman social intercourse – the dinner party.

A stranger visiting in Rome can expect a number of dinner invitations. This is neither charity nor simple hospitality. Invitations are issued because dinner is a good way to investigate a new arrival and whether he and his dinner host might enjoy a mutually beneficial relationship of

some kind (*amicitia*), or because the stranger is so exotic that he might entertain his fellow guests.

On receiving such an invitation, closely question the bearer. He will be expecting this and will have been primed on what to say. Check, for instance, whether this is a *cena*, a full multi-course dinner, or a *symposium* – a drinking party with some snacks. If a *cena*, inquire whether the drinking will be 'Greek style' (i.e. heavy) as this might necessitate a litter for the homeward journey. Dress will be a tunic if dining informally, a sort of dinner tunic called a *synthesis* for more formal meals, but not, unless a very formal occasion indeed, a toga.

Guests are expected to bring their own napkins along, usually a large one. The Romans use forks almost exclusively for cooking and serving food, and eat mostly with their fingers. Given their predilection for spices and sauces, dinner can get very messy indeed. At the end of the meal, guests are generally invited to take home any leftovers which particularly appealed to them, so a napkin may also be called into service as a sort of doggy-bag.

As a rule, respectable ladies do not get

invited out to dinner on their own, though they may attend or host them with their husbands. Instead ladies have morning get-togethers with their friends.

Dinner parties seldom run late – not surprising since the diners may expect to get up an hour or so before dawn. Romans are unequivocally morning people who think nothing of putting in a few hours' work before breakfast, or of arriving at someone's house at sunrise to do business. Schoolchildren setting out from home, tradesmen opening their shops and the bustle of household slaves wake most people at an early hour, so by the time the early afternoon arrives most Romans are ready to pass the hottest hours of the day with a quiet siesta.

After that they head for the baths. In the past most Romans had a full bath every market day (i.e. every nine days), but in these deca-dent times most people have a soak at least every second day or so. After lying about in the *caldarium*, the hottest of the baths, they cool down with a dunk in the *tepidarium*. Then – at about the tenth hour of the day – they are ready to dine.

After arriving, and changing from street sandals, guests are greeted by the *tricliniarcha*, a sort of ancient maitre d', and conducted to the room which is his special charge – the *triclinium*, or dining room (though in some older or less well-appointed houses, meals are still eaten in the atrium). Because dining forms such an important part of Roman social life, the furnishings are as sumptuous as the host can arrange. There will probably be a mosaic on the floor, perhaps wittily showing food already dropped, or a hunting scene. But don't be surprised by a skull, or even a complete skeleton or funeral scene. The Romans feel it adds piquancy to life if, while enjoying it to the full, they remain aware of its macabre alternative.

The best dining rooms are open on one side, perhaps (if the host is far enough up the hills) offering a view of the city, or if not, at least of the house's own modest garden. Frescoes on the walls will generally have a garden or country theme, so the diners' imagination might take them out of the city walls to that dining utopia, a woodland glade somewhere in the Arcadian hills. For all the room's elegance, the host probably does not dine there every day, but in a smaller room with his wife and children, and probably also a few favoured freedmen. While the head of the household may

> *The stomach bug hit me after a banquet at Lentulus' place. . . . I had carefully abstained from the oysters and lampreys, yet was done in by a beet*
>
> CICERO, *LETTERS TO HIS FRIENDS* 7.26

> *With Jews and Syrians and Egyptians and Romans, is it possible that the opinions of all of them are right in respect to food?*
>
> EPICTETUS, *DISCOURSES* 1

If you don't mind lying on Archia's couches, and you don't mind a meatless dinner on modestly sized plates, I expect you as a guest at my home come sunset

HORACE, *EPISTLES* 1.5

Bronze seat.

use a couch on such occasions, it is probable that everyone is seated on mundane and practical chairs or stools.

The *triclinium* is dominated by three large couches arranged with one against the back wall looking out over whatever panorama is on offer, another to its left, and a third to the right. The fourth side is open to allow the diners to enjoy the view, and for servants to approach the table.

Dining couches are large affairs that allow at least three people to recline on them, at 45 degrees to the table, each propped up on his left elbow. If the lady of the household is present at all she will be sitting on a chair, ready to leap back to her domestic duties at a moment's notice.

As guests reach the couches, they are immediately and literally put in their places. The host reclines at the top of the left-hand couch, so that his head is next to the main guest of the evening who occupies the couch against the back wall on the side nearest his host. Two other favoured guests end up on the top couch, and a slightly less favoured pair get to share a couch with the host while the couch opposite is reserved for the remaining three.

Cassius gave a dinner party to which Brutus invited some friends. As the guests were taking their places to dine, in came Favonius, fresh from the baths. Brutus complained that he had come uninvited and ordered the servants to take him to the furthermost couch. But Favonius pushed past them and took station on the middle one.

PLUTARCH, *LIFE OF BRUTUS* 34

The meal will probably start with an offering to the *Lares*, the gods of the household.

Dinner party.

Roman religion is numinous, meaning that in the Roman world small gods inhabit every field, stream and woodland grove, and every houschold has its personalized patron deities who guard the health and fortune of its inhabitants.

The plates and cutlery may vary – they may be wood, clay, pewter, bronze, silver or gold. Some hosts show traditional Roman restraint by serving the food on clay or wooden plates even if they can afford better (at one time it was actually illegal to have too much silver or golden tableware). There is also the rather practical consideration that clay and wood keep food warmer for longer. Look out for the distinctive red clay of Samian ware, by which a host discreetly points out that though the dish is made from clay, it is the best clay money can buy.

Since someone worked out how to blow glass in the mid-1st century AD, glassware has become increasingly common for drinking vessels. The wine served during the meal is *mulsum*, chilled white wine with honey. Use it in combination with the small breadrolls served for that purpose to clear your palate between the highly spiced courses, and leave yourself the capacity to appreciate the finer wines that will be served after the meal.

The first course (the *gustatio*: often eggs, salad with asparagus, salted fish or dormice) is served to the accompaniment of casual chit-chat as the diners sound each other out and note how the host behaves to each.

I happened to be dining with a man … whose elegant economy, as he called it, seemed to me a sort of sordid extravagance. The most elaborate dishes were set before himself and a select few, and cheap scraps of food before the rest of the company.

He had even put out tiny little flagons, containing three sorts of wine, not with the idea of giving his guests a choice, but to make it impossible for them to choose at all. One was for himself and me; the next for his friends of a lower order (for, you must know, he measures out his friendship according to the degrees of quality); and the third for his freedmen and mine. My neighbour at table noticed this and asked me if I approved. I said I did not.

'So what is your method?' he asked.

'I serve the same to everyone, for when I invite guests it is for a meal .. I have brought them as equals to the table, so I give them the same treatment in everything.'

'Even the freedmen?'

'Of course, for then they are my companions at the table, not freedmen.'

'That must be very expensive.'

'Not at all … my freedmen do not drink the sort of wine I drink, but I drink what they do.'

PLINY, *LETTERS* 2.6

The main course is meat, game, poultry, and combinations of each, so smothered in

Silver bowl & ladle.

pungent sauce that it can be hard to determine what is underneath. Depending on the diner's attitude toward delicacies such as snails fattened on milk or well-cooked peacock's brains, this might be considered a blessing. At least the food is served in small bowls on the table so that diners can pick and choose what they eat.

I won't force you to look at girls from iniquitous Cadiz waggling their hips through their lascivious dances; instead little Condylus, my slave, will play the flute

MARTIAL, *EPIGRAMS* 78

RES ROMAE

Most Romans follow 'Varro's rule' which states that the proper number for a dinner party is no less than the number of the Graces (four) and no more than the number of the Muses (nine)

, , ,

According to Roman chefs, to be at its best, a lamprey should be caught while pregnant

, , ,

Rocket was a popular salad dish, perhaps because it was believed to have aphrodisiac qualities

The tone of the evening will be set by the entertainment. There may be readings from the philosophers, cithara music, or poetic works, perhaps even some penned by the host. The Romans take being cultured very seriously and look down on the saucy dancing girls (the best are from Gades, modern Cadiz) who do so coarsen the mood at less highbrow dinners.

Dessert is no afterthought, and may well be an extravagance of sweetmeats, pastries, fresh fruit and nuts.

Afterwards, relax and enjoy the wine, which may be from Gaul, Spain or Italy, and watch the main entertainment of the evening, perhaps a knockabout comedy by the playwright Plautus, or clowns, acrobats, or even some gladiators doing a bit of practice sparring. It is rather bad form to discuss business (that can be done tomorrow, now that the guests have met each other) but philosophy, social observations, and badinage are more than welcome. Two writers, Plutarch and Aulus Gellius, have written whole books about such after-dinner discussions. A convivial affair might only break up at midnight. (Which does not sound too bad, except wake-up time tomorrow is 4 am – and you still have to get home!)

MEETING PEOPLE

O N MEETING A STRANGER A ROMAN IS intensely interested in where he comes from and what he does. How that Roman reacts on a second meeting depends on how much that first conversation has convinced him that the *amicitia* of his new acquaintance is worth having. *Amicitia* is often translated as 'friendship', but the Roman philosopher Seneca is closer to the mark when he calls it 'mutual serviceability'. *Amicitia* means trading gifts and favours with an *amicus* (*amicus* here meaning something between 'friend' and 'useful contact'). Roman society is made up of interlocking networks of such 'friendships', and the favours that Romans do for one another (*beneficia*) are the social currency of Rome.

This can get quite complicated. For example if an *amicus* asks someone to do a favour for another of his *amici*, delicate negotiations follow as to how much this has obliged the *amicus*, and how much the friend's friend. Someone who soaks up too many *beneficia* without returning the favours may gradually slip to the more lowly status of client. Clients are not supposed to return their patrons' benefits in kind, but have different obligations, such as to offer loans if required (many clients combined can contribute a goodly sum), and to gather around the patron in public to show everyone what a large following he has. A good client will show up at his patron's house in the morning to render his *salutatio*, a sort of morning greeting.

At the *salutatio* a client has the opportunity to present his patron with his problems, while the patron will look among his other clients to see who can best provide a solution. So if Fabricus tells his patron that his daughter is looking for a suitable husband, the patron might mention the matter to Statius, a client who has a son of the appropriate age and social station. It helps to clarify the situation by considering that 'patronus' literally means 'big father', but has also been memorably translated as 'Godfather'.

The standard Roman greeting is *ave*, meaning something between 'salutations' and 'hello'. So a Roman meeting a woman called Mary would greet her by saying *ave Maria*. Then he might enquire *quis agis?* This means 'what are you doing?' in the sense of 'what's up?' or 'how are things?'. Goodbyes are said with the word *vale*, and a

> *'But this,' you say, 'would not be worthy of me.' Well, then, it is you who must introduce this consideration into the inquiry, not I; for it is you who know yourself, how much you are worth to yourself, and at what price you sell yourself; for men sell themselves at various prices*
>
> EPICTETUS, *DISCOURSES* I

> *We do not hesitate to dutifully perform services for those whom we hope will assist us in the future*
>
> CICERO, *ON DUTIES* 47

Roman in a hurry might greet a friend with a quick *ave atque vale*, meaning roughly 'hi and goodbye'.

An important Roman has to keep track of so many 'friends' that he has a slave with a good memory by his elbow to mutter the name and a few pertinent details about each person as he approaches.

ROMAN NAMES

NOW, A WORD ABOUT ROMAN NAMES. A Roman man generally has three or four names, and a Roman woman has one. The first name of a Roman man (*praenomen*) is generally used only by intimate friends and family. For example Julius Caesar, Augustus and Caligula were all called 'Gaius' by their mothers. (Just to make life more complicated 'Gaius' is usually abbreviated to 'C'. So Gaius Julius Caesar is written as C. Julius Caesar.)

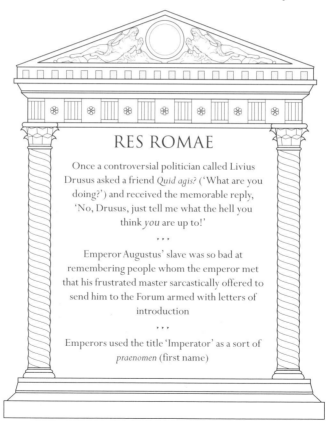

RES ROMAE

Once a controversial politician called Livius Drusus asked a friend *Quid agis?* ('What are you doing?') and received the memorable reply, 'No, Drusus, just tell me what the hell you think *you* are up to!'

, , ,

Emperor Augustus' slave was so bad at remembering people whom the emperor met that his frustrated master sarcastically offered to send him to the Forum armed with letters of introduction

, , ,

Emperors used the title 'Imperator' as a sort of *praenomen* (first name)

I The Temple of Capitoline Jupiter in one of its many incarnations. This picture is from an earlier era, giving an idea of how the Etruscan temple might have looked at the start of the 6th century BC when Rome was still ruled by kings.

II (*Overpage*) Rome as the Romans never saw their city. This Jupiter's eye-view shows the Circus Maximus on the left, with the Colosseum to the right, and between the two the Aqua Claudia bearing water to the Palatine hill. The Temple of Capitoline Jupiter completes the triangle, with the Forum lying along the north part of the line between Colosseum and temple.

III The Aula Regia, throne room of the Caesars.
Built by the emperor Domitian, the room was
designed to awe visitors, no matter from where
(or when) they might be.

IV Theatre of Pompey on the edge of the
Campus Martius. In the background is
the Temple of Venus, the steps of which
conveniently double up as seating for
17,500 spectators, sidestepping the law
against stone theatres in Rome at this time.

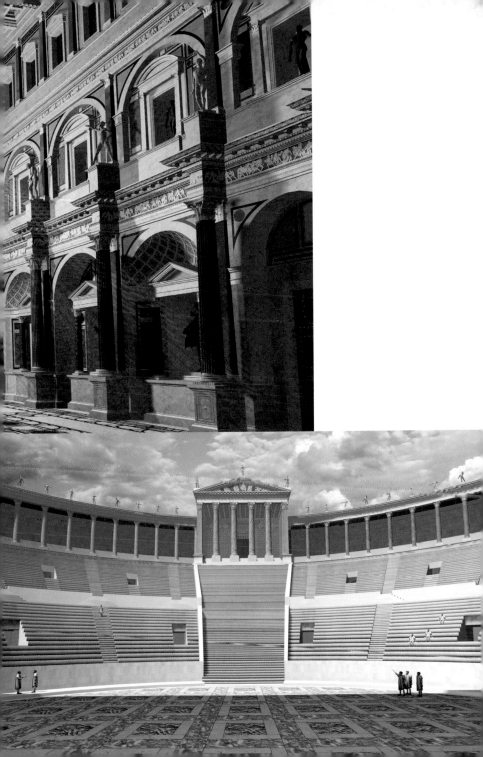

V The Theatre of Pompey was more than a
simple stage. Like the Roman baths it was a full-
scale leisure centre, designed to attract visitors
and impress them with Pompey's importance,
even when there was no one on stage.

VI Temple of Mars Ultor ('the Avenger')
in the Forum of Augustus, flanked with
porticoes which contained statues showing
the great men of Rome, with the Julian
family prominent among them.

The middle name is the name of the *gens*, or clan. These clans can be very large, and two people called 'Julius' might be as remotely related as two MacDonalds are in the 21st century. Because the eldest Roman boy is usually named after his father (e.g. Titus Labienus' son will be called Titus Labienus), the Romans try to reduce the scope for confusion by adding a nickname to the end of the name. These nicknames (*cognomina*) are often based on a personal characteristic. Consider Strabo (squinty), Felix (fortunate), Postumus (born after his father's death) and Caesar (curly-haired). Unfortunately, these nick names might also get inherited, so trying to identify an Appius Claudius Pulcher (*pulcher* means 'pretty') is still difficult as there are several generations of them to choose from.

A man who has been adopted has a name that ends in '-anus' (in Latin *anus* means 'old', especially a wrinkled old woman). For example, Augustus was called Octavian (*Octavianus*) before he became emperor. He originally came from the Octavius family so when he was adopted by Julius Caesar he should have become Caesar Octavianus (though he insisted on being called just 'Caesar').

Women have a single name, taken from their father's *gens*. Julius Caesar's daughter was Julia. Claudius' daughter was Claudia, and Cornelius Scipio's daughter was Cornelia. The flaw in this arrangement does not seem to have occurred to the usually logical Romans. Not only does this land some ladies with rather unlovely names (Cato's daughter was called Porcia), but

A HANDY LIST OF ABBREVIATIONS OF ROMAN PRAENOMINA

A.	Aulus	**M.**	Marcus
Ap.	Appius	**P.**	Publius
C.	Gaius	**Pro.**	Proculus
Cn.	Gnæus	**Q.**	Quintus
D.	Decimus	**Ser.**	Servius
K.	Cæso	**Sex.**	Sextus
L.	Lucius	**Sp.**	Spurius
Mam.	Mamercus	**T.**	Titus
M'.	Manius	**Ti.**	Tiberius

two or more sisters will have the same name, and end up being called (for example) Big Calpurnia, Little Calpurnia and Baby Calpurnia, or Calpurnia first, Calpurnia second, and so on.

THE SOCIAL ORDER

ROME IS AN INTENSELY HIERARCHICAL society. Everyone knows their place, sometimes quite literally. Anyone sitting in the Colosseum where they do not belong could end up as part of the entertainment. Certain seats are reserved for senators, others for equestrians, and so on right down to the seats at the top back, which are for women and slaves. Essentially, the Roman social order from bottom to top goes like this: slaves, foreigners, freedmen, general citizens, equestrians, senators, emperor. It's more flexible than this though – some freedmen are immensely rich and important, and the emperor is also a senator. At the other end of the scale, house slaves look down on field slaves, and native-born slaves despise barbarian imports.

SLAVES

ON MANUMISSION A FREED SLAVE becomes a freedman (or freed-woman) and a junior member of the family that freed him. For this reason, although a freeborn citizen technically outranks one of the emperor's freedmen, the imperial freedman is a junior member of the impe-rial family, and emphatically someone to stay on the right side of. The freedmen of a

'How then shall a man endure such persons as this slave?' Slave yourself, if you will not bear with your own brother, who has Zeus for his creator, and is like you a son from the same seeds and of the same descent from above? But if you have been put in any such higher place, will you immediately make yourself a tyrant?

EPICTETUS, *DISCOURSES* 1.13

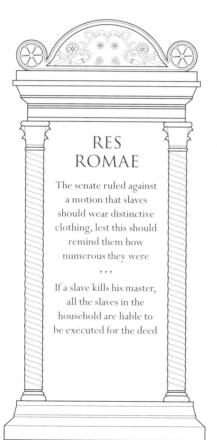

RES ROMAE

The senate ruled against a motion that slaves should wear distinctive clothing, lest this should remind them how numerous they were

. . .

If a slave kills his master, all the slaves in the household are liable to be executed for the deed

Roman citizen automatically become Roman citizens themselves.

While a non-citizen seeking Roman nationality can't just marry a Roman since nationality does not change even after marriage, becoming a Roman's slave and getting freed will do the trick. Of course, the would-be citizen has to really, really trust the Roman to whom he's selling him-self, but this racket happens all over the empire.

The ambiguous relationship between Romans and their slaves is clearly shown by the famously severe Cato the Censor. He called slaves 'talking tools' and advo-cated selling them off before they became elderly and an expense to maintain. But he not only freed several of his slaves, he even married the daughter of one of his freed-men. (Under Roman law incidentally, an ex-master cannot force his freedwoman to marry him – unless he freed her for that very purpose.)

Be cautious in dealing with slaves, and remember that the Romans regard slavery

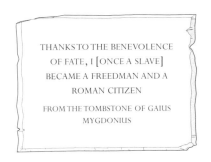

my slaves will also have a taste of freedom ... in my will, I've left Philargyrus a farm. As a bonus he inherits another of my slaves — his current girlfriend.

SOLILOQUY OF TRIMALCHIO IN
PETRONIUS, *SATYRICON* 71

FAMILY

A ROMAN FATHER HAS ALMOST AS MUCH power over his own family as he does over his slaves. Quite literally, as no one has ever repealed the old law that a father can only sell his son into slavery three times. The power of a father is such that if he wishes to whip, starve, exile, or even in extreme cases kill his children then the law is powerless to stop him.

Fortunately, as in many states where the social order is more powerful than the legal system, a father needs to make what at least his fellow Romans would consider a good case for his actions, or find himself friendless for life. (This is actually even worse than it sounds, for a Roman arranges his business as well as his social life with his friends, relies on them to club together to help him when he is in trouble, and depends on them for the mutual exchange of favours by which the entire city functions.)

Therefore, with domestic problems, as with almost every other important decision he makes, the head of a Roman family will, by a kind of social reflex action, first call together a council of his most trusted friends and lay the situation before them. The opinion of the friends is not binding, but at least the father will have a clear idea

as an unfortunate affliction which might happen to anyone.

Before being rude to someone because he is 'only a slave', remember that he might also be a good friend of his master — some slaves even go on to become the adopted children or heirs of their former owners. Yet Rome abounds with examples of extreme brutality, callousness and sadism. This is a different age with different standards.

My friends, slaves are also human beings, and drank mother's milk with the rest of us, even if bad luck has hit them hard. But if my luck holds,

Slave boy.

of what others might consider the right thing to do. An invitation to such a council is a great honour, but an outsider will usually be invited only in the capacity of 'expert witness'. He might for example be doing business in a field in which the outsider specializes, or one of his freedmen may have asked permission to marry a daughter of that nation. In such a case, witnesses should stick to the facts, and not offer an opinion unless directly asked.

Among the important distinctions within a family are *agnati* (blood relatives of the father) and those who are *sui iuris* (independent under the law). Roman law has an odd perspective here, as even the 60-year-old son of an 80-year-old is totally dependent on his father under the law. In theory he can own no property of his own, and is compelled to obey his father implicitly in all things. The domestic strains which can result from this can be seen by the Roman horror of parricide, which is literally the worst offence it is possible to commit. (Though the authorities like to insist that treason to the emperor comes first!)

What gladiator, what thief, what assassin, what parricide, what forger of wills, what cheat, what debaucher, what spendthrift, what adulterer, what abandoned woman, what corrupter of youth, what profligate, what scoundrel can be found in all Italy, who does not swear that he has been on terms of intimacy with Catiline?

CICERO, *SECOND ORATION AGAINST CATILINE* 4

'You parricide' is a favourite insult which even senators are not above hurling at each other, though if the insult were a genuine accusation, the killer would find himself sewn into a leather sack with a dog, a cock, a viper and an ape (since these unfortunate animals are thought to embody the vices – savagery, ingratitude, etc – which led to the crime). The killer would be violently beaten, then dropped, still in his sack, into the Tiber. Parricide, incidentally, includes the murder of grandfathers, and possibly of mothers, while killing an actual father is patricide.

Now we have got that out of the way, remember that, by and large, Roman families are generally harmonious affairs. This is partly because of the huge social pressure on the father that this should be so, and partly because of the father's extensive powers to make it so. Furthermore, a husband's relations with his wife are harmonious for no other reason than divorce (like marriage) is a civil union which either party can withdraw from without social or religious sanction. (Though here too, a daughter will need her father's permission, which is why in

It is utterly important that children are raised correctly, even if this means harsh discipline

SENECA, *ON ANGER* 2.1

Roman law assigns to the father absolute power over his son

PHILO, *EMBASSY TO GAIUS* 4.22

So, Rufus, you say that your rabbit is badly cooked, and yell for your whip. Why would you rather cut up the cook than your dinner?

MARTIAL, *EPIGRAMS* 3.94

Roman comedies an angry wife sends for her father at the first sign of a domestic bust-up.)

Cicero writes to his friend Atticus, whose sister is married to his brother, about a lunchtime squabble:

RES ROMAE

Roman girls, especially among the aristocracy, marry young – sometimes when just into their teens

, , ,

A good dowry is about the equivalent of a father's annual income

, , ,

Adopted children have the same rights as any other children in a Roman household

, , ,

When a new baby is born it is laid at its father's feet – if the father picks up the baby it can live, and if ignored the baby is taken away to die from exposure

, , ,

Children are named about nine days after birth

, , ,

Brothers and sisters are educated together at home when they are young. Though boys get a better education than girls, some women are very well educated indeed

Quintus [Cicero's brother] said gently, 'Pomponia, why don't you invite the women, and I'll see to the men?' As far as I could see, his words and expression could not have been more polite and reasonable. But she, in front of everyone, burst out, 'Me? I'm just a stranger here.' I assume she said that because … she was not asked to make the luncheon arrangements. … We all lay down to lunch except her. Quintus sent some food to her – she sent it back. To sum up, I don't think my brother could have been more reasonable and patient, or your sister more bitchy. There were other things which I won't say here, even though they made me want to puke, since my brother seemed to overlook them.

CICERO, *LETTERS TO ATTICUS* 5.1.3–4

To no one's great astonishment, the unhappy pair eventually divorced. Yet this couple too were once part of a wedding party such as any visitor may encounter in the streets of Rome during a visit. There will be the traditional shouts of *talasio*

from the wedding guests, and the bride in her elaborately knotted girdle and wearing a saffron veil. Since ingenious and extremely filthy jokes are traditionally bandied about on these occasions the bride's veil is perhaps to hide her blushes. (Or maybe to conceal her enjoyment!)

Those in the vicinity may join the wedding party in singing verses such as,

You there, slave boy
Once your master's favourite in bed
Though you have lost his love
Pass round the nuts to the other lads

[nuts are thrown about like confetti on these occasions]

and then the rousing chorus,

Oh! Hymen Hymenaeus!
Hymen Hymenaeus!

SHOPPING

Where to Shop · Changing Money
What to Buy · Aediles

HOPPING, EVEN IN THE CAPITAL OF the world, is a rather hit-and-miss affair. Rome has an impressive array of foodstuffs, and these are widely available. Likewise specialist shops cater for particular needs, such as the perfume sellers on the Vicus Unguentarius. However, many other goods are produced by specialist craftsmen who may or may not have the materials on hand, or who may follow their own idiosyncratic schedules. For example, wine can be purchased in quantities from a cupful in a *caupona* to a boatload at the emporium, but if you are after a particular type or vintage, you might have to wait until a shipment comes in. Most Romans develop relationships with tradesmen they deal with often, so strangers are at a disadvantage.

> *I ask the price of greens and flour, and ... as the sun sets, I'm off home for a dinner of leeks, chickpeas and flatbread*
>
> HORACE, *SATIRES* 1.6

WHERE TO SHOP

You have to produce some goods that retail with a 50 per cent mark-up. So don't act so disgusted at the kind of merchandise only permitted across the Tiber [freshly tanned and evil-smelling leather], or think that there is an important difference between perfume and hides. Profit smells sweet, no matter what you are dealing in.

JUVENAL, *SATIRES* 14.200–5

ASK A ROMAN ABOUT SHOPPING, AND she (shopping in Rome is generally done by women) will probably do a quick mental count up to nine. This is because the best variety and freshest foods are generally found at the *nundinae*, markets which are held every ninth day (which is why they have this name).

In much of Roman Italy you can only do your shopping when the *nundinae* are held. In metropolitan Rome some markets are open every day, but those market gardeners, cheesemongers and shepherds who live more than 15 miles from Rome cannot make a daily trip into the city and still have time to farm. Nevertheless, in a world without refrigeration, Roman housewives want their goods as fresh as possible, so it remains convenient for sellers and buyers to meet every ninth day.

Not only are products grown closer to Rome in great demand, but they tend to be snapped up very quickly. Also, because the profits from market gardening are so immense, those living close to Rome concentrate on this. Farmers living further from Rome often produce less perishable goods – cured meats, sausages, preserved fruits, honey and cheeses or articles made from leather, wood or wool.

So the *nundinae* continue to thrive. The farmers arrive before dawn and set up their stalls in streets which are designated as market streets. These are then closed to regular traffic. (This practice is set to continue for another two millennia, and is a regular event in most 21st-century Italian towns and cities.) For the shopper, working out when to buy at a *nundina* requires fine calculation. Popular articles go quickly, but those who wait until the end of the day (markets close at sunset) can find a farmer who will offer a rock-bottom price to avoid hauling his unsold goods home again.

For those who cannot wait eight days for market day to come around, the emperors have arranged for permanent markets to be set up to complement the *nundinae*, and as an added bonus these are comfortably sheltered courtyards out of the weather. These market places are called *macella*, and are fascinating places to wander about.

After all those things which a human needs to live on have been collected in one place, and the place is given a building for it, this is called a 'macellum'

VARRO, *LINGUA LATINA* 5.147

A stall in a *macellum* tends to cost the stallholder more than one in a street market, and consequently the goods are both more expensive and generally better quality. The concentration is still on food. An average Roman spends about 50 per cent of his income on food, and takes a keen interest in both the quality and price. Substandard fare receives vociferous disapproval. The playwright Plautus complains about...

...fishmongers, who jog into town on boneshaking nags and offer fish so far past their sell-by date that they empty the entire hall with their stench ... and the butcher who robs mother ewe of her little darlings, but still palms his customers off with mutton while pretending it is lamb freshly killed as they ordered. And the mutton! That's usually a tough old ram.

PLAUTUS, *THE PRISONERS* 813–819

Despite Plautus' complaints, *macella*, with dedicated areas for butchers' produce and waste disposal, are slightly more hygienic places to sell meat than the street markets, so many prefer to get vegetables, sausages and cheese at the *nundinae*, and then pop into the *macella* to pick up a couple of hares, some thrushes, or even a good fillet of wild boar. (Many hunters sell their catch in the markets, though boar are also reared on the farm for sale in Rome.) Fish are rarer, as Juvenal explains in a manner startlingly familiar to those living 20 centuries later:

Food stall.With a population of around a million, Rome needs a huge amount of fresh food. If bread is scarce, expect riots. Even Emperor Claudius was pelted with mouldy crusts once when supplies ran low.

The waters around our coasts have been fished out, yet our greed remains rampant. To fill the markets our nets sweep the inshore waters bare ...hardly one fish is allowed to reach full size.

JUVENAL, *SATIRES* 5.93–6

Two of the largest *macella* are the Macellum Magnum on the Caelian hill (dedicated by the emperor Nero in AD 59) and the Macellum Liviae near the Esquiline. But perhaps the best shopping in Rome is at Trajan's Forum on the Quirinal hill. Leave the towering column built in AD 113 by Trajan to celebrate his conquest of Dacia (later Romania) for another day (p. 122). Instead slip between the Greek and Roman libraries flanking the column and duck through the row of archways which divides the austere world of imperial administration from the bustling, everyday world of commerce. Note that the wall doing the dividing is immensely strong and

I wouldn't want to be Florus, strolling around the taverns and picking up fat fleas in the cookshops

EMPEROR HADRIAN TO HIS OLD TUTOR

thick, because the separation of business and administration is more than theoretical. On the one side is a market with quick-roasted foods and a mass of hugely flammable goods, and on the other libraries and law courts with irreplaceable scrolls and papyri. The wall ensures that any disaster which strikes the market stays there.

The market itself is a marvel of contemporary architecture. Though the Romans use concrete with unrivalled flair, on this occasion the concrete is hidden behind brick. Apollodorus, Trajan's architect, made the core of each wall from concrete mixed with rubble, and split his bricks down the middle to save costs on the facing. The result is five huge, honey-coloured terraces marching 125 feet up the Quirinal hill like a giant's staircase.

Each terrace contains over 40 shops, with an arcade in front of each. These arcades are relatively narrow, and difficult to navigate when packed with shouting, jostling humanity which appears to be all elbows and sharp-edged shopping. The shops themselves are relatively spacious, each about 12 feet across with their entire facade open to the public.

Some are eateries and bars. Others offer to grind or process the citizens' corn dole which is distributed from imperial offices on the fifth terrace level. Other shops offer goods from every corner of Rome's vast empire and from points well beyond.

bench – a *banca* – is later to give its name to the entire profession. The money-changer will check that coins have not been 'sauced' (made from copper with a thin layer of silver plated on to the surface), and will carefully check the weight. Older coins can lose weight through innocent wear, but unscrupulous individuals also practice 'clipping' – paring small amounts of metal off the sides of every coin that passes through their hands until they eventually end up with enough precious metal to sell as a small ingot.

CHANGING MONEY

THOSE WHO HAVE BROUGHT THEIR OWN funds to Rome, rather than cashing a letter of credit, will make a money-changer the first point of call. (In some *macella* you will find money traders operating at the the centre of the courtyard.) Money is only legal tender if it comes from an imperial mint, and even then not all imperial coinage is recognized throughout the empire.

The money-changer's stall consists of a large bench at which he does business. This

WHAT TO BUY

SADLY THE PROUD ROMAN COINAGE HAS become increasingly debased over the centuries, and older coins change hands at a premium. The basic comparison table of coins is shown below.

To give you some idea of what this is worth, a Roman soldier gets an annual salary of 450 *denarii*, but various gifts, subsidies and bonuses besides. A town house

BASIC COMPARISON OF COINS

As – a small bronze coin; might buy a half-dozen grapes from a generous shopkeeper

Dupondius – made of brass; worth two *asses*

Sestertius – also a brass coin, and a standard unit of price, often abbreviated to *HS*; worth four *asses*

Denarius – a silver coin which is the standard measure of currency; worth four *HS*

As *of the emperor Vespasian, c. AD 71.*

Obverse: Aecetia, goddess of fair dealing (the inscription reads 'The fairness of Caesar').

in a good area will set the buyer back about half a million *denarii*, and a pint of mediocre wine about a *sestertius*. The price which everyone watches very carefully is that of grain. The Roman pleb is very dependent on grain (the average Roman consumes about two pounds of wheat bread per day), and displeasure at high prices is marked with riots and unrest. After a good harvest, expect to pay about 5 *denarii* for a *modius* of grain. A *modius* is close to 2 gallons, and will produce about 20 loaves of bread which, given that Roman loaves are about 1 pound each, adds up to exactly 10 days' supply.

With clothing, you will pay about 15 *denarii* for a solid pair of boots or about 20 for a pair of fashionable ladies' slippers. Cloth and clothing are relatively costly, since all fabric is hand-woven. In fact even aristocratic women may cut costs by getting their wool fresh from the sheep and spinning and weaving it themselves. If cost is not an issue, those wanting to push the boat all the way out can spend over 100,000 *denarii* a pound for top quality, purple dyed silk, bearing in mind that half a dozen human beings or a pet lion might come for the same price.

No one in Rome knows where silk comes from. This mysterious cloth is imported from the East, from outside the boundaries of the empire. An inquisitive Syrian merchant called Maes Titianos followed the Silk Road back through Nabatea and Arabia through Parthia but finally gave up at the 'stone tower' in Central Asia (probably in modern Uzbekistan). The Romans do know of China. Chinese records speak of a visit from merchants from the emperor An'tun (probably Antonius Pius or Marcus Aurelius), but trade between the two empires is done through intermediaries.

Spices and ivory are regularly imported from India, and even from the fabled island of Taprobane (Sri Lanka) where there has been a trade mission since the time of the emperor Hadrian. Cotton, pearls, ivory, cinnamon, pepper and frankincense: all are available at a price, though if you want the best, leave Trajan's Market and go to the shops along the Via Sacra, the road leading into the Forum of the Romans. Walk gently, as this is probably the most expensive retail street in the world. For lower prices and more everyday commodities, try the Vicus Sandaliarius and other roads running parallel to the Via Sacra on the Esquiline side.

Made conspicuous by my gifts, may she walk through the city in fine silks woven on gold bands by the women of Cos. Let dyes of African crimson and purples from Tyre compete for her favour

TIBULLUS, BOOK 2.3.51–53; 57–8

Going up the Argiletum? ... Look for me there. Atrectus – that's the shopkeeper's name – will hand me down from the first pigeon hole (well, maybe the second). One Martial, smoothed down with pumice stone and finished in purple, 5 denarii to you, guv

MARTIAL, *EPIGRAMS* 1.117

WEIGHTS, MEASURES & TIME

1 *pes* (plural *pedes*) − 1 foot of 12 *unciae* (inches); the Roman foot is about half an inch shorter than the modern measurement

1 *semis* = 6 *unciae*

1 *dupondius* = 2 feet

1 *passus* = 5 *pedes*; literally, while walking, the point where one foot leaves the ground to where the next foot is put down afterwards

1 *mille passus* = 1 mile, or more precisely 1,618 modern yards

1 *iugerum* = 1.246 acres; a *iugerum* was about the amount of land that could be ploughed in a day (subdivided, an *uncia* = 1/12 of a *iugerum*, or *triens* = 1/3 of a *iugerum*)

The standard measure of a volume was the *amphora*, which is about 25 litres, or 7 US gallons

The *libra* = 1 pound, which is why the £ in the pound symbol is the shape it is; the crossbar is to avoid confusion with the Latin L for 50 (*libra* is also why scales, and hence the zodiacal symbol, have that name)

1/12 of a pound is an *uncia*

The Roman day has 12 equal hours. However, those 12 hours are from sunrise to sunset, so a day in midsummer has hours up to 30 minutes longer than average, and hours at night are correspondingly shorter. In winter the situation is reversed. The Romans measure time by the sun and with candles and water clocks (or even little portable sundials) so the changing of the hours is a matter of opinion. 'Easier for two philosophers to agree than two clocks,' remarked Seneca. Nobody bothers much about minutes...

The *Argiletum* is particularly good for books.

A feature of commercial life in Rome is auctions. Anyone with goods to dispose of might go to a designated commercial area and set up his pitch, but most leave this job to professional auctioneers. (Though the emperor Caligula himself once raised funds this way − not unexpectedly getting excellent prices from his terrified audience.) The household goods thus disposed often include slaves. Most slaves are sold only a few times in their lives, so the experience is both nerve-wracking and humiliating for them.

An auctioneer will start by explaining the slave's abilities and previous experience, if possible adding (or inventing) glowing testimonials from the previous owner. Highly qualified slaves get the best

Eros almost cries as he looks at the murrine cups, the boys, the classy citronwood. ... He'd like to take the whole lot home, and so do the others. Some who, dry-eyed, laugh at his tears, secretly share them

MARTIAL, *EPIGRAMS* 10.80

prices (the millionaire Marcus Crassus used to train slaves himself for this purpose) and *vernae*, slaves born in captivity, command high prices. Since sexual use of slaves is an everyday occurrence, the physical beauty of the slave also has an important effect on the price. The cheapest slaves are captured barbarians, mostly suited only for work in the fields. During the Republic, Sempronius Gracchus captured so many prisoners in Sardinia that 'Sardinians for sale' remains the Roman expression for 'two for a penny'.

A girl of none too nice renown,
The kind you often see down town,
An auctioneer had up for sale,
But bidding languished, seemed to fail,
And so, to prove her pure and sweet,
And almost good enough to eat,
While she pretended to resist,
He drew her closer to him, kissed
Her on the mouth, three times, then four,
To prove his point so much the more.
You ask what good this kissing did?
The highest caller withdrew his bid.

MARTIAL, *EPIGRAMS* 6.66

AEDILES

MARKETS ARE TIGHTLY REGULATED IN Rome, which is unsurprising, given the volatility of the Roman mob and the associated hazards of overcrowding and fire. Buyers and sellers must have the *ius commercii*, the right of a citizen or favoured ally to trade goods in Rome. Magistrates called Aediles and their officials have the job of checking that merchants have legal title to their wares, and that the weights and measures have not been cunningly shortened or lightened. The authorities encourage buying through markets because sales can be properly regulated (and taxed). In the tale of his adventures in Greece, Apuleius tells of an encounter with one of these market officials:

I was leaving the market when an old acquaintance from Athens happened to pass by. ... I asked him how he came to be dressed as in official garb, and followed by servants with rods ... He said, 'I'm a market official, and if you want something for supper, I'll make sure you get it.'

I thanked him heartily, but said I'd already got some fish. But when Pithias saw the basket with the fish in it, he shook it and demanded how much I had paid for my sprats. I told him that I had bargained the price down to 20 HS from the fishmonger. At that, he hauled me back into the market and demanded that I point out the vendor. I showed him the old man sitting in his corner and Pithias, in his capacity as a market official, flew at him.

'Is this how you treat strangers, and my friends at that? Selling fish at this price, when the lot are worth a single as? ... Well, my overcharging friend, you know my job, and how I punish offenders.'

He took my basket and threw the fish to the ground. Then he told one of his watchmen to trample them under his feet. This done, he asked me to leave, saying that the shame of the reproach should be enough for the old scoundrel. I went off, feeling somewhat stunned (and without any supper).

APULEIUS, *THE GOLDEN ASS*, 1.24–5

As well as regular markets, there are fairs. These often coincide with Roman games or religious festivals, when many out-of-towners have made a special trip to the city. The fairs often have a theme and attract specialist merchants, such as live-stock dealers or slave traders. For example, those going to Rome for the midwinter solstice should remember that an exchange of gifts is traditional at the Saturnalia festival. So look out for the Sigillata fair on the Campus Martius in mid-December, where books, plates, statuettes and other potential gifts are available. 'There is a huge amount of selling just before the Saturnalia,' remarks the writer Macrobius, 'and it goes on for days on end.'

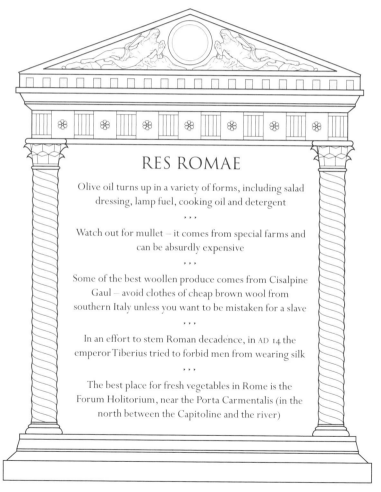

RES ROMAE

Olive oil turns up in a variety of forms, including salad dressing, lamp fuel, cooking oil and detergent

, , ,

Watch out for mullet – it comes from special farms and can be absurdly expensive

, , ,

Some of the best woollen produce comes from Cisalpine Gaul – avoid clothes of cheap brown wool from southern Italy unless you want to be mistaken for a slave

, , ,

In an effort to stem Roman decadence, in AD 14 the emperor Tiberius tried to forbid men from wearing silk

, , ,

The best place for fresh vegetables in Rome is the Forum Holitorium, near the Porta Carmentalis (in the north between the Capitoline and the river)

LAW AND ORDER

Praetorians · Urban Cohorts
Vigiles · Crime · Law Courts
Prison · Punishment

VI

OME DOES NOT HAVE A POLICE FORCE. This is perfectly normal for an ancient city, and it means that there is a clear distinction between 'law and order', which is the job of the government, and 'crime prevention', which is the job of the community. The system works because, despite appearing to strangers as a swarming anthill of humanity, Rome is actually a mosaic of tightly knit communities in which everyone knows everyone else's business. Also, a draconian punishment system cuts down on offenders – and does so literally.

PRAETORIANS

NY DISCUSSION OF LAW AND ORDER IN Rome has to begin with the Praetorian Guard, since any Roman knows that the city would be much more law-abiding and orderly if the entire accursed unit was lined up and marched, cohort by cohort, into the Tiber.

The Praetorians' highly appropriate insignia is a scorpion, because they were organized into their present form by the emperor Tiberius, who was a Scorpio (the Romans pay great attention to their horo-

scopes). The job of the Praetorians is to protect the emperor, and even today, when the emperor leads Rome's armies against the enemy he is accompanied by his *cohors praetoria*. According to the average legionary this is a squad of over-privileged popinjays totally undeserving of their higher pay and special privileges.

Do the Praetorians, who get two denarii a day – and who retire after 16 years – face the same dangers? They are happy enough to do sentry duty in Rome, yet here we are among savage tribesmen, the enemy visible from our very tents.

DECLAMATION BY A MUTINOUS FOOT
SOLDIER IN TACITUS, *ANNALS* 1

And that was in the days when the Praetorians still had a reputation as an elite unit. Things started going downhill when the Praetorians decided to make Claudius emperor in AD 41, and there was nothing the senate could do to stop them. Because the Praetorians make up the largest military unit in the vicinity of Rome, the emperors depend on them for their protection. But, as the Romans say, *quis custodiet ipsos custodes?* ('who is going to guard the guards?'). The real loyalty of the

Praetorians is unswervingly towards their pay packet. Emperors have for centuries kept them loyal by offering larger and larger rewards. When an emperor comes to the throne, his first act is to give the Praetorians a huge one-off payment called a donative.

Very recently, the Praetorians totally disgraced themselves and Rome. Because they felt that the emperor Pertinax had not paid them a large enough donative, they

Laborious marches and military discipline were equally distasteful to men accustomed to sailing the lakes of Campania, or swanning off to the cities of Greece

THE PRAETORIANS FALL OUT WITH THE EMPEROR GALBA IN TACITUS, *HISTORIES* 1.23

killed him and took his head back to their barracks on a pole. Then they *auctioned* off the empire to the highest bidder, which turned out to be a senator called Didius Julianus. This got them officially disbanded by the emperor Septimius Severus, but he has recruited his own guards who are Praetorians in all but name, though they are stationed a bit further out of Rome.

The common people loathe Praetorians for their arrogance and brutality.

Become a soldier and you'll have it made — most of all in that get-rich-quick brigade, the Praetorians.... If some poor civvy gets beaten up by one of you, he won't even dare to go to court and show the magistrate the teeth you've knocked out, his face swollen into a purple lump, and the remains of an eye that the doctor is hoping to save.

JUVENAL, *SATIRES* 16.1–2; 8–12

By now you will have got the idea. If you come across any Praetorians, don't avoid them like the plague. The plague is most certainly the better option.

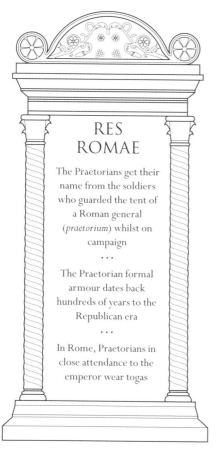

RES ROMAE

The Praetorians get their name from the soldiers who guarded the tent of a Roman general (*praetorium*) whilst on campaign

· · ·

The Praetorian formal armour dates back hundreds of years to the Republican era

· · ·

In Rome, Praetorians in close attendance to the emperor wear togas

URBAN COHORTS

THOUGH STATIONED IN THE SAME CAMP as the Praetorians, members of the Urban Cohorts have half the pay and twice the popularity. When the semi-demented emperor Commodus recently unleashed his cavalry on the Roman people for daring to protest about his ham-fisted rule, it was the Urban Cohorts who beat the horsemen back.

The Urban Cohorts are under the command of a high-ranking senator, the City Prefect. The quality of these prefects varies alarmingly and has done so ever since their first commander, Valerius Corvinus, resigned his post in 13 BC with the disarming admission that he had not the faintest idea what he was supposed to be doing.

The job of the Urban Cohorts is to keep public order. When the crowds get carried away with excitement after a rousing day at the races, or looters start piling in after a fire, the Urban Cohorts will step in (unless the looters are Praetorians, as has been known to happen). When the Urban Cohorts step in, it is an excellent idea to step out, since the basic premise of the Cohorts is that anyone in a riot is a rioter and rioters can't disturb the peace if they are unconscious or dead.

VIGILES

THESE ARE IN PART THE NOCTURNAL equivalent of the Urban Cohorts. In recognition of the fact that Rome is a less turbulent place by night, the Vigiles prefer clubs to sharp-edged weapons. Unlike their diurnal counterparts, the Vigiles are stationed in small barracks around the city, the quicker to react to gangs of drunken party-goers getting violent on the way home, or reports of nocturnal cut-throats on the prowl.

Those guilty of misdemeanour by night may be hauled off to a holding tank as a preliminary to facing the commander of the Vigiles in the morning, since this commander also has the powers of a judicial magistrate.

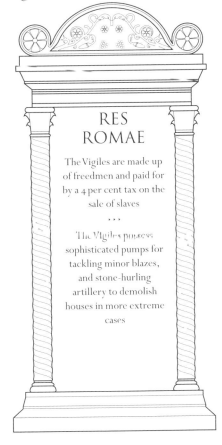

RES ROMAE

The Vigiles are made up of freedmen and paid for by a 4 per cent tax on the sale of slaves

• • •

The Vigiles possess sophisticated pumps for tackling minor blazes, and stone-hurling artillery to demolish houses in more extreme cases

Greatly as the Romans appreciate the Vigiles keeping the public peace, this is something of a sideline to their main job, which is firefighting. The public is more ambiguous about this role. Roman buildings are generally too combustible for the traditional bucket-chain to be useful against anything more than minor blazes, so the Vigiles seldom bother. Instead they make a lightning assessment of how fast the fire is spreading, and contain it by tearing down the buildings in the way. They have highly-trained specialists to rip off roofs, flatten walls, and yank anything flammable from the wreckage, and they do this at breathtaking speed.

Since the owners of the premises concerned seldom agree with the Vigiles about the optimal point in the street for demolition to take place, they tend not to be as appreciative of this sterling public service as they should be.

CRIME

SINCE THE GOVERNMENT OF ROME IS concerned only with public order, the job of fighting crime is left to Joe Citizen. And his neighbour, and everyone else in the city.

Every person in Rome is familiar with notices of the type to the right. It may seem surprising that Rome functions at all without a police force, but the citizens operate their own form of a neighbourhood watch, and have a summary way with potential offenders. Life in

Someone has taken a copper pot from this shop. I offer 65 HS for its return, or 20 HS if anyone can tell me where it is

CIL 4.64

Rome is lived very much in the public eye, so furtive crime is much harder to get away with. Ill-gotten gains need to be explained, not least because the victims of theft loudly proclaim their loss and often offer substantial rewards for information. It is very common for the victim to establish the identity of an offender after a cursory inquiry. After this, the patronage system comes into play.

To see the system in operation, let us imagine a visitor has brought with him to Rome a fine cloak of Gallic wool. He puts it aside in a tavern due to the heat of the day, and moments later it has gone. He cannot call the police, because there are none. The landlord of the tavern, recognizing a visitor to the city, is emphatic that the problem does not concern him. The visitor returns to his lodgings angry and cloakless.

His host is distressed, not so much by the loss as by the treatment of a guest under his roof. He contacts a friend who is the friend of the patron of the tavern owner. The Aediles might be mentioned, since they have the power to close badly run drinking establishments. Under pressure, the patron of the tavern admits that a regular – Lucius, from the street of the Lampmakers – is rather light-fingered, and Pupina, one of the waitresses, has heard that he is flaunting some new finery.

The host has a short discussion with his major-domo, who in turn briefs five burly household slaves. The little group sets off from the house and in due course returns bearing a cloak. Not a little concerned that he may have ruined the day of a perfectly innocent Lucius, our visitor examines the cloak, recognizes its distinctive pattern, and proclaims ownership. If by mischance Lucius has quite coincidentally come legally into possession of an identical cloak, he will even now be making indignant representations to *his* patron, who will send a messenger around so that things can be sorted out in a civilized fashion. If all else fails, the matter will go the the law courts.

LAW COURTS

A FORM OF FREE STREET THEATRE MUCH appreciated by the cognoscenti is the process of hounding someone to trial. Under the Roman self-help system of law enforcement, once an appointment has been booked with a magistrate, the plaintiff has to make sure that the defendant turns up in court. Obviously, the weaker the defendant's case, the more reluctant he will be to present himself.

To apply pressure, the plaintiff might hire a specialist to sit under the defendant's window, or on the street outside his door, and howl ingenious insults and imprecations to the delight of passers-by and the mortification of his victim. Should the object of these attentions step out of doors, he will be followed down the street by his persecutor, who will loudly inform all and sundry of the villainous nature of the accused, and his lily-livered refusal to defend himself before a judge. A truly determined plaintiff will hire his insult-mongers to work in shifts, and after a few wakeful nights the neighbours will be applying their own pressure.

Since personal reputation (*dignitas*) matters immensely to a Roman, it is a rare citizen who can take this sort of treatment for long, especially as the longer he puts off his day in court the more everyone will assume him guilty, and treat him accordingly.

A Roman civil lawsuit has a certain brutal elegance. It comes in two parts. First, plaintiff and defendant appear before a magistrate – generally a Praetor, but for smaller or commercial cases, an Aedile. The Praetor is a busy man, and he is not going to hear the case. Instead he establishes that there *is* a case, and that both parties are *sui iuris* – subject to Roman law. A visitor may not be. (Slaves' children and madmen aren't either.) This is one reason why the host has made the issue between himself and the light-fingered Lucius.

The Praetor checks his list of local worthies who might be called on to act as judges, and appoints someone that everyone agrees on, or at least someone that the litigants cannot offer a credible reason for not wanting.

The Praetor then gives the formula, which defines what the case is about and what the judge has to find out. In this example, the formula runs like this:

'If the plaintiff [Lucius] can show that the cloak is his, and he has been unfairly deprived of it, the defendant [the host] must return the cloak and pay damages. If the defendant can prove that the cloak was stolen by the plaintiff [Lucius], then the charge of theft stands against the plaintiff.'

The Praetor sets a date for the trial three days in the future. Unless there are public holidays or religious festivals in the way, this is the usual time between the two parts of the lawsuit. Lucius is very likely to back down before the actual trial. Firstly, as the plaintiff, the burden of proving his case rests with him. Secondly, the host may be found, at worst, to have acted on a misunderstanding, and being guilty of a civil offence he can only be fined (this is true even if his slaves inflicted grievous bodily harm on Lucius while retrieving the cloak – Rome can be a rough town). But if Lucius can be proved to have stolen the cloak, this is a criminal offence and he might be whipped, sold into slavery, or sent to the mines (and fined as well).

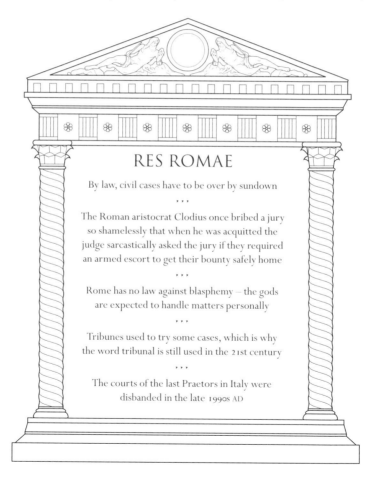

RES ROMAE

By law, civil cases have to be over by sundown

. . .

The Roman aristocrat Clodius once bribed a jury so shamelessly that when he was acquitted the judge sarcastically asked the jury if they required an armed escort to get their bounty safely home

. . .

Rome has no law against blasphemy – the gods are expected to handle matters personally

. . .

Tribunes used to try some cases, which is why the word tribunal is still used in the 21st century

. . .

The courts of the last Praetors in Italy were disbanded in the late 1990s AD

Lictors. These servants of a magistrate precede him in public, clearing the riff-raff from his path. They carry the fasces (rods and — outside Rome — an axe), symbols of the magistrate's power to punish.

However, the fate of Lucius would be decided at a second tribunal, since criminal cases go to a jury trial, and are altogether more serious affairs than civil suits. Note also, that once the two litigants have appeared in front of the Praetor, the case will go to judgment unless both parties withdraw, since if anyone fails to turn up later without giving a good reason (being dead or dying are the only really acceptable excuses), then the judge will usually find in favour of whoever bothered to show up.

It is a basic precept of Roman justice that both the trial and the punishment should be public (though women, for modesty's sake, are generally executed behind a curtain). This leads to some colourful and grotesque results in the amphitheatre, but it also means that in the

*What use are laws when money alone is king
And poverty can never carry the day?*

PETRONIUS, *SATYRICON* 14

forums of Rome magistrates can be seen hearing cases in front of a jury. Rome may be a military despotism, but a citizen's rights under the law are generally respected, and nowhere more than in the public courts. Of course, Romans being Romans, meticulous legalism is punctuated with public flamboyance and theatre. Everyone remembers the moment when the lawyer of an accused general dramatically ripped the toga from his client's shoulders to reveal his many battle scars, then spun him around, to show that not a single one of these scars was on his back. The accused and their families also make other plays for public sympathy, the women donning mourning clothes, and the men sporting black togas and going unshaven to emphasize their plight.

PRISON

I F CAUGHT WRONGDOING IN ROME IT may come as a relief to know that the Romans do not normally use prisons as places of punishment (though relief may be tempered by the knowledge of what that alternative is). Despite its wealth by ancient standards, even Rome does not have the financial resources to keep large numbers of its population unproductively isolated from society. So prison is generally where they keep people while deciding whether to release them, fine them or do something much nastier. Aristocrats do not even suffer imprisonment this long. They are kept in the houses of their peers, who guard them politely until the emperor decides their case.

The prison ... is in the middle of the city, overlooking the Forum

LIVY, *HISTORY OF ROME* 1.33

Whilst the occasional defaulting debtor might be locked up by his creditor as a means of squeezing the cash out of him, this is done in a private lock-up. Imperial Rome has a 'give them liberty or give them death' philosophy for her citizens which means that the city has but one prison of note. This is right in the middle of the city, overlooking the Forum with the temple of Mars Ultor nearby. Damp and gloomy as this prison is, its historical value makes it worth a visit, though it is infinitely better to go as a tourist than as an inmate.

Repulsive and terrible on account of neglect, dampness and smell

SALLUST ON THE TULLIANUM, *CATILINE* 55

The prison is generally known simply as the *carcer* (from which the English word 'incarcerate' originates), and it is divided into two sections. The upper chamber is roughly quadrilateral. An inscription there states that it was restored in AD 21, but it remains a cold, gloomy and bad-smelling room. This makes it a huge improvement on the lower section, an abandoned cistern called the Tullianum. (*Tullius* is an ancient name for a spring of water, which contradicts the argument of the Christian sect that one of their leaders, called St Peter, brought this spring into existence so as to baptize his guards.)

The Tullianum is a conical windowless chamber of rough-hewn tufa, the only entrance to which is a hole in the floor of the room above. Prisoners were flung through this hole into the prison, and on occasion left there to starve and rot.

When the renegade Numidian king Jugurtha was thrown into this cell in 104 BC, his first comment to his guards was how cold it was.

For all that the site is to become a church in later centuries, it is uncertain whether St Peter did actually enjoy Roman hospitality here. But those implicated in the Catiline conspiracy were certainly imprisoned within its walls before they were strangled on Cicero's orders, and anyone of Gallic blood will certainly want to visit the site where the most famous Gaul of antiquity,

Vercingetorix, met his end. Vercingetorix united most of Gaul in a heroic attempt to defeat Julius Caesar, but was captured and made his final public appearance at a traditional Roman triumph, which involved him being paraded through the Forum before being returned to the Tullianum to be strangled, while Caesar enjoyed a magnificent banquet a few hundred yards away on the Capitol.

PUNISHMENT

PUNISHMENTS IN ROME depend on two things – what the criminal has done, and who he is. The vast majority of offences are covered by a fine. The Romans have a detailed set of tables, listing types of injury, and how much compensation each is worth. The Roman magistrates have servants called Lictors who carry the *fasces*. These are bundles of rods symbolizing a magistrate's power to administer physical chastisement (though magistrates have not been allowed to flog citizens since the Late Republic). Outside Rome the *fasces* also feature an axe, showing that magistrates can and do exercise the power of life and death over non-citizen provincials.

Any Roman sentenced on a capital charge can appeal to Caesar – the right famously exercised by St Paul. This is one of many advantages of being Roman, and what makes exile, and the accompanying loss of citizen privileges, so fearsome. Technically, exile is not a punishment but an escape from punishment. The condemned is welcome to remain in Rome – some of the lower orders are forced to remain in Rome – and face death instead. Aristocrats get beheaded, citizens are generally strangled, slaves and non-citizens may be flogged, burned, thrown to wild beasts, crucified or otherwise imaginatively disposed of.

There is also a lesser punishment, *infamia*, which is a public record that a citizen is such a generally bad lot that, though permitted to remain in Rome, the right to vote, take on debts, or speak in a public assembly is withdrawn.

Slaves can be punished arbitrarily by their owners, though their rights under the law are slowly increasing even as those of the very poorest are declining. It was once the case that a convicted thief became the slave of the man he stole from, but these days a thief is more likely to end up in the mines, or if the theft was violent, in the amphitheatre. Which brings up another interesting aspect of Roman life – justice as entertainment.

> *Those who break into a temple by night to cause damage or steal are to be thrown to the lions. Those who steal from a temple by day are condemned to the mines*
>
> PAULUS, *OPINIONS* 5.19

> *'You have been condemned', they told him*
> *'Is it banishment or death?', he asked*
> *'Banishment'*
> *'And my property?'*
> *'Is not confiscated'*
> *'Let's go then, gentlemen, for it seems we must have supper in Aricia'*
>
> EPICTETUS QUOTING THE STOIC AGRIPPINUS, *DISCOURSES* 1.1

ENTERTAINMENT

Colosseum ⟩ Circus Maximus
Theatre ⟩ Prostitution & Brothels

VII

AS MIGHT BE EXPECTED OF A CULTURE allegedly based on bread and circuses, the Romans take playtime very seriously. Entertainment is available at every level, from the board games scratched on the pavements to spectaculars costing millions in the amphitheatre. However, the broad range of activities which the Romans put under the name of 'fun' shocks many cultures both contemporary and later, which see nothing remotely entertaining about the slaughter of defenceless prisoners or the forced prostitution of 14-year-old girls.

COLOSSEUM

WHETHER OR NOT A VISITOR ATTENDS the games while staying in Rome is a matter of personal ethics. Anyone who considers gladiatorial spectacles crude, brutal and depraved will not be alone. Only a small percentage of the population of Rome attends any particular session of the games. Many do not go because they can't get the tickets, but others just don't want to. Seneca, a philosopher and advisor to the emperor Nero, wrote (in his *Letters* 7.3):

I chanced to drop in on a midday show [at the games], looking for something clever and entertaining, some relaxation in which human eyes could have a break from seeing human blood. It was quite the opposite. All the fights beforehand were acts of mercy in comparison; now all lightheartedness was gone and we were offered nothing but butchery.

Yet, terrible as the arena is, its horrors are offered with a panache seldom, if ever, equalled in human history and the spectacle may yet suck you in. Augustine's *Confessions* (6.8) tell of a friend named Alypius, who avoided the arena,

being utterly averse to and detesting such spectacles. One day by chance he met some acquaintances and fellow students coming from dinner, and they hauled him, kicking and screaming, into the amphitheatre during one of these cruel, deadly shows ... the man he saw fall had taken a wound through the body, yet he himself was struck even more savagely in the soul ... as soon as he saw that blood, he became drunk with the brutality of it all. He could not turn away, but remained staring ... mindlessly delighted with that guilty fight, and intoxicated with the whole bloody pastime.

These days, the gods of Rome do not accept human sacrifice, so gladiatorial games are not part of the religious festivals of Rome. In fact there are not much over a dozen times in the year when a visitor can be fairly sure of catching a gladiatorial show. One such occasion is the midwinter festival of the Saturnalia, since Saturn is the god of the underworld, and gladiator shows are *munera*, offerings to the spirits of the dead.

Town criers announce the games, and soon afterwards little groups form about advertising signs while the most literate person present explains the forthcoming spectacles. 'Before the games, who talks of anything else, either in the home or in the tavern?' asks one writer. Betting on fights is officially discouraged but intense. As a class, gladiators are despised as slaves or criminals (and sometimes work on the side as bodyguards, debt collectors and rent-a-

Nothing ruins your character more than going to these spectacles

SENECA, *LETTERS* 7.2

thugs), yet top gladiators have a sweaty glamour that makes them the superstars of their day.

Even in a respectable marriage, in which a husband traditionally parts his bride's hair with a spear, the ritual is considered especially potent if the spear has at some time been dipped in the blood of a dead gladiator. Juvenal comments on a well-born runaway wife:

And what were the youthful charms which captivated Eppia? What did she see to allow herself to be called 'gladiator fodder'? … A wounded arm gave promise of a discharge, and there were various deformities in his face: a scar caused by the helmet, a huge boil upon his nose, a nasty septic dribble always trickling from his eye. But he was a gladiator! It is this that transforms these fellows into the most beautiful youths imaginable!

JUVENAL, *SATIRES* 6.103–110

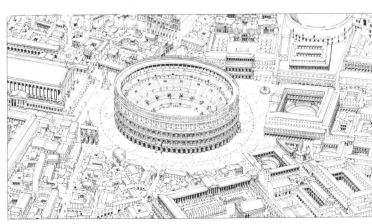

The Colosseum in AD 350. Note Hadrian's temple of Venus and Rome, and Nero's Colossus, which gives the area its name.

THE MOST COMMON TYPES OF GLADIATOR

Dimachaeri – armed with two short swords

Equites – riders with a spear and sword

Essedari – Celtic-style charioteers

Hoplomachi – Greek-style hoplites; often paired with *Mirmillones* or *Thracians*

Laquearii – armed with a lasso

Mirmillones – use a sword and an oblong Gallic shield; often paired with *Hoplomachi*, *Thracians* or *Retiarii*

Retiarii – armed with trident, dagger and net; they fight *Secutores* or *Mirmillones*

Samnites – carry a rectangular shield, helmet and short sword

Secutores – have a shield, helmet and sword; the usual opponents of *Retiarii*

Thracians – have a round shield and curved dagger; they fight *Mirmillones* or *Hoplomachi*

At the 'open dinners' before the next day's fighting, some women flirt shamelessly with the gladiators on display, while hardened gamblers carefully examine the form of their fancies. They cannot approach too closely, because each gladiator is closely supervised by a *lanista* (literally a 'bladesman'), who has trained his man for months or even years for this event. There are four gladiator schools in the city, the largest of which, the Ludus Magnus, is so near the amphitheatre that it is connected by an underground tunnel.

The Colosseum (properly known as the Flavian Amphitheatre) itself is the most imposing stadium on earth. It sits in the valley between the Caelian, Esquiline and Palatine hills, just down the Via Sacra from the Roman Forum, with the triumphal Arch of Titus between. A giant 130-foot gilded statue of the sun god Helios stands beside the amphitheatre and gives the

> *Norbanus arranged a show with gladiators – the whole lot hardly worth tuppence – so old and decrepit that you could blow them over*
>
> PETRONIUS, *SATYRICON* 45.11

name 'Colosseum' to the whole area, rather than to the building itself.

One hundred and sixty four feet high and 656 feet across, the amphitheatre occupies six acres of land. Each level of the distinctive arched tiers of travertine stone is of a different architectural order: the first storey is Doric, the second Ionic, the third Corinthian. Above is another level of concrete faced with brick, and a final level of wood. Pine masts with banners top it off.

With tens of thousands of spectators flooding into the stadium, it is important to approach from the correct angle to begin with. Each ticket is marked with the appropriate entry gate. There are 80 of these gates, with the corresponding numbers at the top of each archway (76 for ordinary spectators, 2 for the imperial family and their retinue, and 2 for the gladiators). Within, the corridors are so wide, and the system of ramps and tunnels so

Gladiators at work. For all its ostentation, note how little protection the armour gives against lethal blows. On the right, a referee parts two combatants with a rod as the losing gladiator holds up his index finger to indicate surrender to the mercy of the crowd.

efficient, that the amphitheatre fills in less than 20 minutes, and afterwards spectators are disgorged onto the street so rapidly that the corridors are nicknamed *vomitoria*.

Spectators cannot just sit anywhere. The best view is from the podium, but this marble terrace is reserved for senators, visiting ambassadors, the priests of the sacred colleges and others of the great and good. On the southern side of the podium

CELADUS THE THRACIAN, THREE TIMES CROWNED VICTOR, THE YOUNG GIRLS' HEART-THROB

, , ,

CRESCENS, WHO CATCHES MAIDENS IN HIS NET BY NIGHT

GRAFFITI TESTIFYING TO GLADIATORIAL SEX APPEAL

is the imperial gallery where the emperor sits. Beside this gallery sit the Vestal Virgins, and behind that, 20 tiers of seats are reserved for the equestrian order. The rest is divided into three parts: the *immum*, for wealthy citizens and their guests, the *summum* for poorer citizens, and the very top, wooden level (standing room only) is for women. Despite the 50,000–80,000 people packing the stands, from almost every angle the arena is surprisingly close and personal, its elliptical shape helping to bring spectators closer to the action. The floor of the arena is one of the most blood-soaked places on earth. At least 100 humans and more than twice that many animals have died for every single one of its 48,440 square feet.

While no games have exactly the same pattern, the first event will probably be a parade of the participants. If any of these hurl missiles into the crowd, try to grab one. This is the Roman equivalent of the national lottery, with prizes ranging from a good meal to a mansion to an elephant or a broken pot. Don't expect women gladiators, as these were recently banned, though female dancers and acrobats strut their stuff between the bloodier acts.

The amphitheatre offers one of the few chances to see a Roman emperor at close range. This is where emperor and people interact, and the interaction reveals much about the state of things in Rome. Popularity is the best guarantee of an emperor's safety, so every emperor seeks ever more exotic and fabulous beasts to fascinate the crowds. On display are ostriches, crocodiles, leopards or even hippos, many of which will die in the next event – the *venatio*, or hunt.

For the *venatio*, a carefully-contrived forest may rise from the floor of the arena, and animals appear as if by magic. The apparently solid sand covers an underground complex of cages, tunnels and ramps, where levers and counterweights constantly bring new sights to view and take away the old. Some hunts pit different animals against each other, bears against bulls, or lions against elephants. More often human fighters take on the most ferocious wildlife in the Mediterranean basin.

The appetite of the arena has wiped out entire species in some areas. Even during the Republic, Cicero wrote:

About the panthers, I've instructed the usual hunters to do their best. But the beasts are in remarkably short supply ... they are reported to have decided to leave this province and go to

OCEANUS, FREEDMAN,
WINNER IN 13 BOUTS,
VICTOR

ARACINTUS, FREEDMAN,
WINNER IN 9 BOUTS,
LOSER

ARENA SCORECARD, *CIL* 4.8055

Caria. But the matter is receiving close attention ....Whatever comes to hand will be yours, but what that amounts to I simply do not know.

CICERO, *LETTERS TO HIS FRIENDS* 2.11.2

For Romans nature is threatening, rather than under threat, and the hunt is a reassuring show of human superiority. Animal fighters are professionals, the Roman equivalent of bullfighters, rather than criminals being punished. That punishment, as Seneca discovered, often happens at lunchtime, which may be a good moment to duck out and eat, or simply duck out and save whatever is already in your stomach. The Romans believe that justice should be done as spectacularly and messily as possible.

The *noxii*, public executions, are for the lowest of the low. *Damnatio ad bestias* is for those considered human beasts: poisoners, rapists, bandits and military deserters. The condemned are not let loose in the arena, but usually attached to stakes together with a description of their crimes. Incidentally, being a Christian won't be among those crimes. Persecutions of Christians happen infrequently, and when Christians are thrown to the lions, it is not in the Colosseum.

There will be a dozen or so executions, followed by an equally grim business when the condemned, encouraged by whips and branding irons, fight each other to the death. There is no escape for the victor, who must face fresh opponents until he himself is killed. In a society without police the deterrent effect is powerful, and just as importantly, the spectators are reassured that the evildoers they fear do

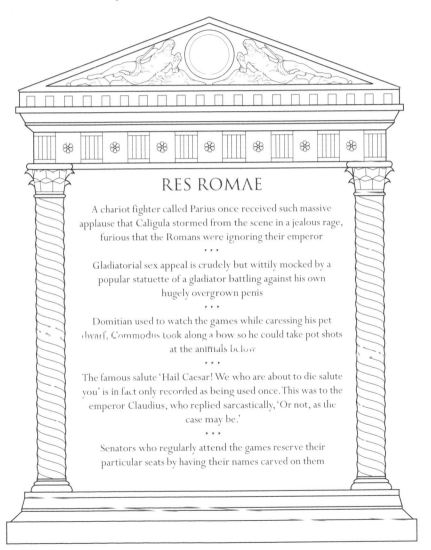

RES ROMÆ

A chariot fighter called Parius once received such massive applause that Caligula stormed from the scene in a jealous rage, furious that the Romans were ignoring their emperor

, , ,

Gladiatorial sex appeal is crudely but wittily mocked by a popular statuette of a gladiator battling against his own hugely overgrown penis

, , ,

Domitian used to watch the games while caressing his pet dwarf, Commodus took along a bow so he could take pot shots at the animals below

, , ,

The famous salute 'Hail Caesar! We who are about to die salute you' is in fact only recorded as being used once. This was to the emperor Claudius, who replied sarcastically, 'Or not, as the case may be.'

, , ,

Senators who regularly attend the games reserve their particular seats by having their names carved on them

indeed on occasion receive just punishment.

After lunch, fresh sand is strewn on the arena floor, and the warm-up fights for the gladiatorial combats begin. These are often comic affairs staged, for example, between clowns and dwarves, and seldom involve bloodshed, let alone loss of life. As the afternoon heat builds, a thousand sailors from the imperial fleet at Misenum swarm over the rigging attached to the masts topping the amphitheatre, pulling over huge sails to shade the audience. These sails are dyed a variety of colours, and the shifting play of light over the audience is a powerful counterpoint to the surreal events in the arena (which is never shaded).

The gladiators appear to a roar of applause. Early bouts might match teams of gladiators against one another, but with popular gladiators the crowds want to give each fight its undivided attention.

Fights might also feature the bizarre *Andabatae*, who fight each other wearing eyeless helmets in a deadly game of blind man's bluff. A gladiator's armour protects him from minor wounds while leaving him exposed to killing thrusts. A roar of *habet*, ('he's caught one!') tells when a man has been struck, while *peractum est* ('that's done it!') indicates a killing blow.

A gladiator unable to continue the fight will raise his index finger – appealing for mercy, not from his opponent but from the *editor*, who stages the games. Naturally, the *editor* takes his cue from the emperor, who generally follows the opinion of the crowd. A judge wielding a long stick separates the fighters until the decision is reached. A popular gladiator who has fought well will get roars of *mitte* ('let him go!') while for others the crowd may chant *iu-gula! iu-gula!* (kill! kill!).

If the decision is for death, the crowd falls silent. A gladiator should die bravely. The defeated fighter bows his neck, kneels and grasps his opponent, now his executioner, by the thigh to steady himself. The executioner plunges his sword point downward through the vertebrae of his victim's neck down into the heart.

The 'thumbs up' gesture is actually deeply ambiguous since it mimes this downward killing strike (try stabbing straight down with an imaginary sword and see for yourself) and note also that sheathing a Roman sword involves turning the hand over so that the thumb points downward toward the body. Therefore those offering a supplicant gladiator an upturned thumb may not be doing him any favours.

Once killed, a gladiator is dragged through the dread exit gate of the dead, the Porta Libitinensis, there to be stripped of his weapons and armour, which will be returned to his comrades-in-arms.

The victor receives his prize purse for the fight, and a palm leaf signifying victory, perhaps even a gold crown. Collectors circulate with trays for spectators to add a few coins of their own. Afterwards everyone settles for the next bout, or to watch a circus turn featuring trained animals or acrobats. Whilst totally at ease with slaughter, the Romans combine openness with prudishness in matters sexual and there is little blatant eroticism on display.

There is however at least an erotic sub-text to the dramas of the Colosseum, as is immediately obvious from the numerous prostitutes waiting for the crowd to stream out into the evening air. The blatant couplings in their rented cubicles under the Colosseum's arches (*fornices* in Latin) have given rise to the word 'fornicate'.

CIRCUS MAXIMUS

THIS IS THE POET OVID TAKING HIS DATE to the chariot races:

He's a fortunate fellow, the charioteer you back; he has been lucky enough to get your interest. I wish I had his chance. I'd be at the starting-post in a moment, and I'd let the horses run clean away with me. Here, I'd shake the reins about their necks, here, I'd let them feel the whip, then round I'd go within a hair's breadth of the turning-post. ...

The Circus Maximus.

Why do you keep trying to shuffle away from me? It's impossible because the seating forces us to sit close together. That's an advantage I owe to how the Circus is set up. But you, you sitting on the other side of the lady, watch what you're doing. Stop leaning on her like that. And you there, behind her, stop sticking out your legs and letting your knobbly knees dig into her back.

Careful, darling, you're letting your hem drag on the ground. Pull it up a little, or I shall have to do it for you. ... What would happen if I saw your legs? ... From what I've seen of you, I can well imagine those other charms that you keep so well hidden under that elegant dress.

The Praetor's just given the signal. The four-horsed chariots are off. I see your favourite, and anyone you favour is a winner. The horses seem to know what you want. Oh gods, look how wide he takes the turning-post. You miserable specimen, what the devil are you up to? Now you've let a competitor with cornering ever so much tighter get ahead of you. What are you playing at, imbecile? What's the use of a woman's backing you?

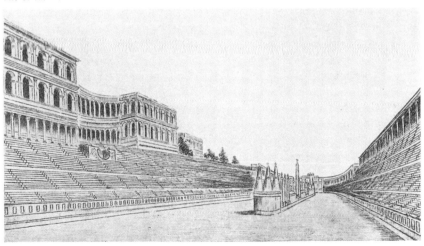

For heaven's sake, left rein hard, go on, pull! Oh,
our man's an idiot. Come on, Romans, have
him back, let's see your togas wave. See?
They're calling him back. But mind they
don't muss your hair, waving their togas
about like that. Come shelter your head in
the folds of my toga.

Look, now they're starting again, the bars are
down. Here they come, in their various colours,
driving like mad. . . . He's won. Now I must see
what I can do. Ah, a smile, my sweetheart, and
that look holds promise. That's enough for here.
You'll give me the rest elsewhere.

OVID, *AMORES* 3.2

THE CIRCUS MAXIMUS

The Circus is 3.5 *stades* in length [just over 2,000 feet] and 4 *plethra* [400 feet] wide. A canal has been dug, 10 feet in depth and width, to receive water on the two longer sides and one of the shorter sides. Behind this porticoes, three storeys high, have been built. The lowest storey of these has stone seats, gradually rising one above the other, as if in the theatre. The two upper storeys have wooden seats. The two longer porticoes are continuous, being linked by the shorter one, which is crescent-shaped, so that all three form a single portico as in an amphitheatre, though this one has a circuit of 8 *stades* [almost 5,000 feet] which can hold 150,000 people. The other short side is left uncovered and contains the roofed starting-boxes for the horses, which are all opened simultaneously by a single rope. Outside the Circus there is another portico of one storey which has shops and then apartments over these. In this portico there are entrances and ascents for the spectators at every shop, so that the countless thousands of people can come and go without congestion.

DIONYSIUS OF HALICARNASSUS,
ROMAN ANTIQUITIES 3.68

If gladiator fights are the Romans' passion, chariot races are their obsession. Nothing can match the atmosphere as about 200,000 tightly packed race fans fervently roar on the best riders in the world as they throw their tiny chariots through death-defying manoeuvres. For excitement and spectacle the Circus is indeed 'Maximus'.

This is one of Rome's oldest places of entertainment. It was established in the time of the kings, almost a thousand years ago, and has been rebuilt several times since. In 50 BC Julius Caesar expanded the track to its present length of 1,968 feet. (The Circus is about 738 feet wide, divided down the centre by a low barrier called the *spina*.)

The whole edifice was reconstructed almost from the ground up after the disastrous fire which started here in the time of Nero, and the current building is mostly the work of the emperor Trajan, who gave the stands a complete makeover and added 5,000 seats.

You'll get for a year what a chariot driver earns in a single race

JUVENAL TO A SCHOOLTEACHER, *SATIRES* 7

Charioteer in action.

Unlike the rigid seating plan at the amphitheatre, seating at the hippodrome is mostly a matter of arriving early and scrummaging through the crowd. For major events, such as the Ludi Romani in September, many Romans prefer to watch the races while picnicking on the south slopes of the Palatine which have a view over the Circus. Within, the best seats are found at the western end (the blunt side) near the imperial box, though for once, the emperor does not have the best view. This is from the *pulvinar*, a sacred box for the statues of the gods which are led there by the magistrates in a procession from the temples. In Rome, *everyone* goes to the races.

That 65-foot-high obelisk on the *spina* was originally raised in Heliopolis, Egypt, in around 1250 BC. (It will be moved from the Circus in AD 1587 to remain thereafter in the Piazza del Popolo.) During the race one of the seven stone eggs along the *spina* is removed when each lap is completed. Those with seats at one end of the track can't see the eggs, and they look instead for the bronze dolphins that dip their heads to do the same job. Agrippa, Augustus' admiral, put these up, to remind the public that he was admiral of the fleet which defeated Antony and Cleopatra in 31 BC.

The charioteers are in teams: red, white, green and blue. Almost everyone, in Rome and in the whole empire, supports one or another of these. Betting is intense, and support is passionate. Just the suspicion that a race has been fixed is enough to cause rioting. A curse tablet has been found on which the writer calls on the demons of the underworld to

... torture and kill the horses of the Green and White factions, and kill and utterly crush the breath from the bodies of the charioteers Clarus, Felix, Primulus and Romanus.

CRESCENS, DRIVER FOR THE BLUES, BORN IN MAURITANIA, DIED AGED 22

EPITAPH OF A CHARIOTEER, *CIL* 6.10050

Usually 12 chariots start the race from staggered boxes so that the outside teams are not at a disadvantage. 'Single entry' races are where each team enters a single chariot. Given that dozens of charioteers die every year in the races, calling on a demon is hardly necessary. For these young men, the maxim 'live fast, die young' is a literal truth. Their chariots are little more than tiny platforms on wheels, and crashes are frequent, spectacular, and often fatal.

Scorpus, darling of the roaring Circus, wildly applauded, but short lived. Snatched away by spiteful fate when only 26 years old. Fate counted by victories, not by years, and that made you an old man. What injustice! You have been robbed of your youth, Scorpus, and all too soon have harnessed the dark horses of death. Time and again you hurried to cross the finish line — why does it now have to mark the limit of your life?

MARTIAL, *EPIGRAMS* 10.53

Occasionally the Circus is used for bloodier exhibitions, such as the execution of Christians, though these executions happen more often at the Circus of Nero in the Vatican fields, not coincidentally near the burial place of one of Christianity's greatest figures, St Peter.

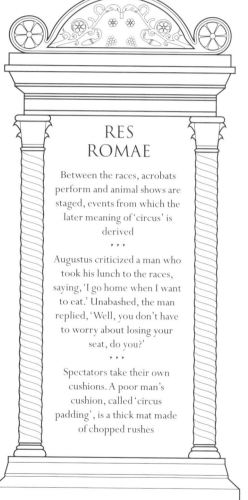

RES ROMAE

Between the races, acrobats perform and animal shows are staged, events from which the later meaning of 'circus' is derived

، ، ،

Augustus criticized a man who took his lunch to the races, saying, 'I go home when I want to eat.' Unabashed, the man replied, 'Well, you don't have to worry about losing your seat, do you?'

، ، ،

Spectators take their own cushions. A poor man's cushion, called 'circus padding', is a thick mat made of chopped rushes

THEATRE

THOUGH MUCH APPRECIATED BY THE intelligentsia, drama in Rome is something of a Cinderella as an entertainment form.

The first time I tried to present this play, I was competing for an audience with some well-known boxers, and a tightrope walker as well ... So I tried an old stage-hand's trick. I presented

the show a second time. This time it worked. I kept my audience right up to the end of Act One. Then someone spread the word that gladiators were about to perform, and my audience surged away in a mob, almost climbing over each other for the best spots.

TERENCE, *THE MOTHER-IN-LAW* 21–34

Those looking for Greek tragedies had best look for a private showing, though be warned: people who appreciate Aeschylus or Sophocles like to do so in the original Greek (nearly all well-educated Romans are almost bilingual). Fortunately, there are also some lively Latin writers, such as Terence and Plautus, who combine literature with knockabout comedy in a style later copied by a certain Mr Shakespeare. The joy of such plays is that they can be presented as elegant stage productions (which you can watch from a comfortable seat, although in the playwrights' time the Romans insisted on taking their entertainment standing up). Alternatively, the same scenes can be staged by two or three itinerant actors with minimal props. Not by coincidence, most of the action in these plays is in the street outside a house, so a small troupe can take over a few yards of street frontage and put on an *ad hoc* performance.

Theatrical events are staged on market days and public holidays, so the actors expect their audiences to be in a carnival mood and play up to the crowd. The plots are a timelessly familiar mix of improbable coincidences, mistaken identities and moral dilemmas, but with the added twist that gods or demi-gods may make an unexpected appearance at any moment. Indeed, the plot device of a god suddenly being winched down onto the stage to

Stretched overhead, the saffron and purple canopy flutters on the cross-beams, sending colours rippling across the rich scenery and crowded auditorium

LUCRETIUS,
ON THE NATURE OF THINGS 4.75–80

Comic actors playing stock characters. A furious stick-wielding father is restrained from getting angry with his spendthrift son. Note the stylized masks and scenic backdrops.

resolve everyone's problems at the last moment is so hackneyed that the expression *deus ex machina* has come to mean 'an instant and miraculous solution'.

Pantomimes are virtually plot-free presentations hung loosely about some mythological event, and feature music, dancing, violence and nudity. To the disgust of the elite, they are enormously popular with the masses.

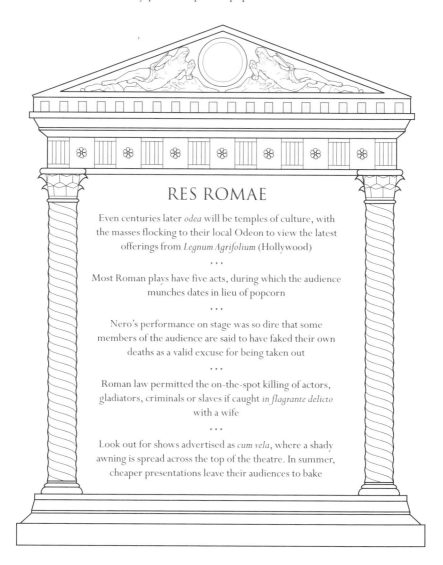

RES ROMAE

Even centuries later *odea* will be temples of culture, with the masses flocking to their local Odeon to view the latest offerings from *Legnum Agrifolium* (Hollywood)

, , ,

Most Roman plays have five acts, during which the audience munches dates in lieu of popcorn

, , ,

Nero's performance on stage was so dire that some members of the audience are said to have faked their own deaths as a valid excuse for being taken out

, , ,

Roman law permitted the on-the-spot killing of actors, gladiators, criminals or slaves if caught *in flagrante delicto* with a wife

, , ,

Look out for shows advertised as *cum vela*, where a shady awning is spread across the top of the theatre. In summer, cheaper presentations leave their audiences to bake

Those who prefer Euterpe to Terpsichore (i.e. the muse of lyric poetry to the muse of dance) seek out the little covered theatres called *odea* for poetry readings, declamations from great works, or presentations by masters of the lyre and flute. Nero tried his hand at public exhibitions of music in such a setting. He aroused public disgust, not only by his poor performance, but because musicians are just a step above actors. And actors are in turn just a step above prostitutes, and quite prepared to take that downward step if offered the slightest inducement. Which leads us to another very common pastime in Rome – exchanging sex for cash.

PROSTITUTION & BROTHELS

PROSTITUTION HAS A LONG HISTORY IN Rome. The founders of the city, Romulus and Remus, were suckled by a she-wolf; a story that gains credibility with the discovery that the slang for prostitute is *lupa*, and that even in these times, such 'she-wolves' recruit many youngsters for their trade by saving them from death by exposure.

Giton, pale and bloodless, and myself brought to death's door by the harlot's wantonness

PETRONIUS, SATYRICON 2

The streets of Rome contain an astounding and abundant display of explicit erotica in everyday contexts, from obscene wall-paintings in the baths to the bread-seller's loaves shaped as male and female genitalia. Sometimes this is not pornography for its own sake – wine might come in a vessel shaped like an erect male penis, because the phallus is a symbol of health, prosperity, and abundance (but only the seriously inebriated would drink straight from the bottle). However, in many cases, the pictures and carvings mean exactly what they depict.

The Romans are not so much uninhibited about sex as inhibited about different things. The poet Martial, for example, complains that while his girlfriend is an imaginative and enthusiastic bedfellow, she refuses to bathe with him naked, or even partially clothed. The Greeks like to think of the Romans as so inhibited about the sight of sex that they are incapable of performing with the lights on.

Prostitutes are everywhere in Rome. They have their *fornices* under the arches of public buildings, including, as we have seen, the Colosseum. They are especially thick around temples, which affords Christian writers some biting analogies. Some prostitutes are named after their preferred habitat, such as the *bustuariae* – 'grave watchers' – who practise in cemeteries, sometimes within the tombs themselves. At the top of the profession are *meretrices*, often companions to the cream of society. *Lupae* occupy a 'she-wolves' den' or *lupanaria,* a full-time brothel. Street girls are *scorta erratica* ('wandering sluts'), and at the bottom of the heap are the *diobolariae*, literally 'two-bit' whores. As with most times and cultures, the work is dangerous and degrading, and in Rome many prostitutes are quite literally sex slaves.

Even these *noctilucae* ('night-moths') prefer to perform the act itself in the privacy of a cubicle. These 'cribs', little rooms with a single stone bed and a straw mattress, are at least as common as toilets at the back of many drinking establishments.

The laws of supply and demand mean that venal sex in Rome is cheap. A street-walker can be had for the price of a loaf of bread, and even a higher-priced brothel girl costs two or three hours' wages for an average workman. With brothels, note that a *stabulum* can be either a normal boarding house or a brothel, so do check before booking a room.

Brothels are denser in particular areas of town, not through official restrictions, but because that is where the customers are. The Subura is a notorious red-light area, and many of the houses along the Via Patricius near the Circus Maximus carry the graffito *hic bene futui* – a coarse comment on the quality of the sex on offer within.

Most brothels open at about 2.30 in the afternoon (which may be why prostitutes are sometimes called 'ninth-hour girls'). The mistress is called a *lena*, and generally takes payment at the door in exchange for tokens indicating graphically which services have been purchased. The *belle du jour* waits in her cubicle behind a patchwork curtain, with her name, prices and special-

> *I want a girl who will let me have it both ways for an extra* denarius
>
> MARTIAL, *EPIGRAMS* 9.32

> *If some young man ends up sleeping with her, well really, is he her corrupter or her customer?*
>
> CICERO, *PRO CAELIO* 20.49

ities listed beside the doorway. In keeping with Rome's brutally patriarchal ethos, customers are males only. Ladies are assumed to take their pleasures more discreetly with gladiators, slaves and male bath attendants, or, if really hard up for cash or sex, as payees rather than payers. Nor are many of Rome's poor averse to making a bit on the side, and part-time prostitutes are less subject to social approbation, and just as importantly, do not pay the tax that full-timers have to.

But be cautious of graffiti with comments like the one saying 'Claudia, the mill-girl, gives excellent oral sex for very reasonable prices'. This might have been written by a disaffected boyfriend, and Claudia could be less than thrilled at the arrival of a hopeful customer.

There are just a few sexual diseases that the tourist needs to be aware of. The risk of herpes, chlamydia and other genital infections rises as customers go downmarket. (Upper-class establishments employ a shuttle service of waterboys from the fountains so the girls can wash down after each customer. Top brothels are directly plugged into an aqueduct, indicating an institution that is well connected in every way.) For the upper classes, it's embarrassing to patronize a brothel, but because brothel-creeping is for the common folk, not because it is immoral. In fact, many senators and even the city authorities make a good income as direct owners or franchisers of such establishments. Of course teenage males of any class may roll in at the end of a late-night drinking party.

If there's anyone who thinks that a young man should be forbidden from sex, even with prostitutes, he is certainly a man of stern righteousness, but out of touch, and not just with the loose morals of today but even with the rules and relaxations of our forefathers.When was this not allowed? When was it wrong to do what is lawful?

CICERO, *PRO CAELIO* 48

Despite this, in Rome as elsewhere, prostitution and criminality often go hand in hand. Those who succumb to the many temptations on offer should remember that it was the Romans who coined the expression *caveat emptor* – 'buyer beware'!

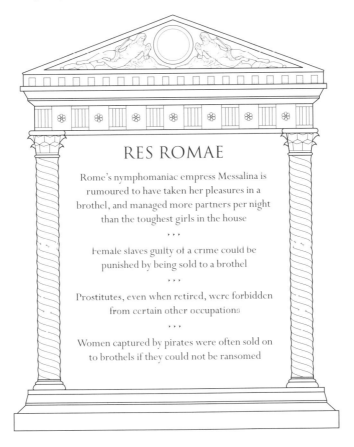

RES ROMAE

Rome's nymphomaniac empress Messalina is rumoured to have taken her pleasures in a brothel, and managed more partners per night than the toughest girls in the house

, , ,

Female slaves guilty of a crime could be punished by being sold to a brothel

, , ,

Prostitutes, even when retired, were forbidden from certain other occupations

, , ,

Women captured by pirates were often sold on to brothels if they could not be ransomed

RELIGION

Temples to Visit · The Pantheon
Religious Festivals

VIII

ROME, OF COURSE, IS THE CITY OF the gods, for without divine patronage, how could Rome have become the mightiest city in the world? Rome swarms with gods – not only does the Roman religion have hundreds of them, but every nation, including Jews, Arabs, Germans, Spaniards and Britons, have each imported their own. Every street has some little shrine, and temples are almost as ubiquitous as taverns.

To find the nearest Roman shrine simply look in the house where you are staying for the *lararia*, a small shrine to the gods of the household where it is traditional to burn as a sacrifice any food that falls to the floor during a meal.

A further set of domestic spirits, the *Penates*, have their place at the hearth, the traditional centre of the Roman home. The chief male of the family, the *paterfamilias,* acts as the priest to these family deities, though one of the consummating rites of a Roman marriage is when the bride sacrifices to the gods of her new family.

Roman religion is based on the *pax deo-*

How can I possibly record in just one section of one book the names of all the gods and goddesses?
AUGUSTINE, THE CITY OF GOD 4.8

rum. Provided that the gods receive their due rituals and sacrifices, they will remain with the community and shelter it. Major deities may indicate that they are peeved about something through prodigies (unusual events such as comets and thunderbolts), floods, plagues and earthquakes, but it is far worse if the gods abandon a city altogether. In fact, the Romans have a rite called *evocatio.* During a particularly tough siege their priests might call on the enemy city's gods, inviting them to abandon their present city for the superior amenities of Rome. It seems to work, though it does add to the multiplicity of Rome's temples.

Provided the gods of Rome are given their due, it doesn't really matter to them whether their worshippers believe in them or not. Having taken part in the official rituals, a citizen is free to worship whatever other deities he pleases. Rome's gods are there to be obeyed and respected, not loved, and they no more mind sacrifices to other deities than the taxman minds people paying other dues elsewhere. Dealing with the gods is an exchange of duties and mutual respect. Confessing a deep love for a particular god is *superstitio* and the person concerned is probably emotionally disturbed.

Because Rome's gods are civic gods, there is no separation between religion and state. The emperor is the chief priest, the *Pontifex Maximus*, while the judge presiding over a law court today might be due to sacrifice a bull to Jupiter tomorrow. A visitor to Rome will certainly see some of these sacrifices taking place. The sacrificial animal is led, garlanded with flowers, to

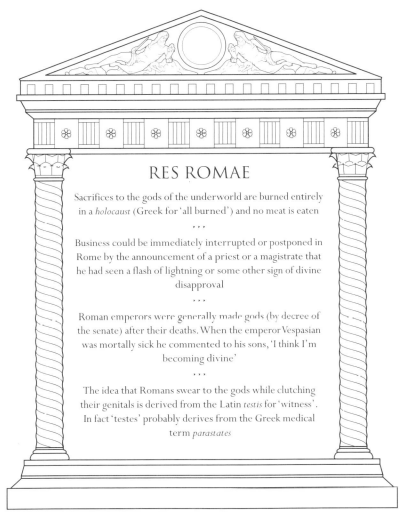

RES ROMAE

Sacrifices to the gods of the underworld are burned entirely in a *holocaust* (Greek for 'all burned') and no meat is eaten

, , ,

Business could be immediately interrupted or postponed in Rome by the announcement of a priest or a magistrate that he had seen a flash of lightning or some other sign of divine disapproval

, , ,

Roman emperors were generally made gods (by decree of the senate) after their deaths. When the emperor Vespasian was mortally sick he commented to his sons, 'I think I'm becoming divine'

, , ,

The idea that Romans swear to the gods while clutching their genitals is derived from the Latin *testis* for 'witness'. In fact 'testes' probably derives from the Greek medical term *parastates*

*Now Caesar's approaching
murder was foretold to him
by unmistakable signs ...
He went to the Senate in
defiance of the omens*

SUETONIUS, *LIFE OF CAESAR* 81

the altar (in Rome altars are outside, in front of the temple) where the priest dedicates it by sprinkling a special flour (*mola*) on its back. The immolated victim is killed, and a priest called a *haruspex* may examine the entrails. Perfectly formed organs are a sign that all is well, while deformities, or an animal that seems to have died unwillingly, are signs of heavenly displeasure.

The sacrificial animal's entrails are burned for the gods, while the other participants tuck into the meat which is left over. This is also sold on the spot, and it is worth buying a steak. It costs slightly more, but what is the price of sharing a meal with a god, maybe even with mighty Jupiter himself?

TEMPLES TO VISIT

THE TEMPLE OF CAPITOLINE JUPITER. The first port of call must be to the Temple of Capitoline Jupiter the Best and Greatest, the temple which is the centre of the state religion. Situated on the Capitoline hill, as the temple's name suggests, Jupiter's is one of the very oldest temples in Rome, allegedly built by Romulus soon after the foundation of the city itself, almost a thousand years ago. To the

Romans this temple symbolizes their city's power and glory. They say that when the foundations were being dug, a human head was unearthed, which the soothsayers interpreted to mean that Rome would one day be the head of the world.

Today the foundations are honeycombed with tunnels packed with dedicatory offerings, statues and treasure. The statues once adorned the roof, but as one of the highest buildings in Rome, the temple is regularly smitten by Jupiter's

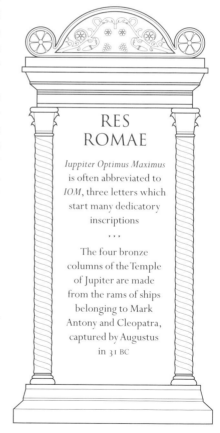

RES
ROMAE

Iuppiter Optimus Maximus
is often abbreviated to
IOM, three letters which
start many dedicatory
inscriptions

• • •

The four bronze
columns of the Temple
of Jupiter are made
from the rams of ships
belonging to Mark
Antony and Cleopatra,
captured by Augustus
in 31 BC

thunderbolts, and the damaged statues are carefully stashed below ground. The current temple is the work of the emperor Domitian, who restored it in AD 82 after it burned down in AD 80, when it had just been rebuilt after being burned down in the civil wars of AD 69, after Augustus had restored it in 26 BC after a lightning strike, although the building he restored was the replacement for the building which burned down in 83 BC. See it while it's still standing!

The temple is awesome. The columns, eight feet wide at the base, are of white marble of a type allowed to no other building in Rome. The doors are plated with gold, and even the roof tiles are gilded. The temple is rectangular, and faces a smidgeon east of due south. It has three *cellae*, individual rooms of the gods, because Jupiter shares his residence with Juno and Minerva. (But look also for a small shrine to Terminus, the god of endings, for of all the gods, only he and that adolescent rebel Iuventas, the goddess of youth, refused to be rehoused from their original temples on the hill when the temple to Jupiter was first raised.) The original statue of Jupiter was of terracotta, and the face was painted red on festival days (which is why, when the emperor rides in triumph to celebrate a victory, his face is painted that way too). Today Jupiter is a massive seated figure, apparently made completely of gold and ivory.

> *Jupiter, I bring to you these spoils of victory, a king's armour, taken from him by a king ... and I dedicate to you this holy precinct*
>
> ROMULUS FOUNDS THE TEMPLE OF JUPITER *c.* 750 BC, LIVY, *HISTORY OF ROME* 1.10

Here at this temple the consuls offer their first public sacrifices, here triumphal processions end, and here all documents dealing with Rome's relations with foreign powers are stored.

THE TEMPLES OF THE FORUM. LEAVING the Capitoline hill, walk down the Gemonian steps, past the Mamertine prison to the Forum. We will examine the Forum in more detail later, but for now, observe the granite columns of the Temple of Saturn, which stands in the north-west corner. After those to Vesta and Jupiter, this building, for the most part of travertine stone, is one of the oldest religious buildings in Rome. It was dedicated in 498 BC, though what is now visible is from a restoration in 42 BC. When the temple was founded Rome was still an agricultural community; and as well as being the husband of Ops (Fortune), Saturn is a god of agriculture. Here too are the bronze tablets of the ancient Twelve Tables, the collection of laws which are the foundation of the mighty edifice of Roman law.

Saturn himself has a statue of ivory, the feet of which are restrained by woollen cords which are only released on his festival day, the Saturnalia, on 17 December.

Opposite the Temple of Saturn stands the senate house, or Curia, which is itself a temple, for the senate can only meet on sacred ground. Within stands a statue of Winged Victory captured by the Romans from Pyrrhus in 272 BC. Legend says that if the statue is removed, Rome will fall soon after. Given that the Romans already dislike Christians, it may not be tactful to mention that Christian emperors will remove the statue in the 5th century AD and that Rome will fall soon afterwards.

Next is the shrine of Vesta, goddess of the hearth, sister of Juno and Ceres (the goddess of crops after whom cereal is named). The shrine was recently rebuilt in AD 191, and has a courtyard with porticoes running around four sides and fountains and pools in the middle. Within Vesta's shrine there is no statue, but instead a sacred flame. Parts of the shrine are forbidden to all but the Vestal Virgins. The Virgins prepare the *mola* (flour) used in sacrifices and tend the sacred flame.

Should the fire go out, this is bad news for Rome, but even worse news for the Vestals, since it indicates that one of their number has been impure. After the guilty Vestal has been found and punished and

I accept you ... as a priestess of Vesta, who will perform the sacred rites as is lawful for a priestess of Vesta to perform on behalf of the Roman people

WORDS BY WHICH THE *PONTIFEX MAXIMUS* INDUCTS A NEW VESTAL VIRGIN

her lover beaten to death, the fire must be re-lit the hard way, by rubbing sticks together. Vestals serve for 30 years, after which they are released from their vows and may even marry. However, it is believed that the jealous gods drastically shorten the lives of such husbands, and as atheists and men with a death-wish make unsuitable spouses, many Vestals stay on, unmarried, at the shrine even after their retirement.

Next comes the mid-2nd-century Temple of Antoninus and Faustina, a marble edifice on a tall plinth preceded by a flight of brick stairs. This temple, dedicated to the emperor Antoninus and his wife Faustina, deserves mention for its extraordinary toughness. Until the 16th century AD, the Roman Forum will stand, mouldering, but largely intact. Then, in an extraordinary burst of Renaissance vandalism, much of it will be torn down by Christian barbarians as building material for churches, especially the new Vatican. However, the columns of this temple will withstand all efforts to topple them, although their tops will evermore bear the deep scars where the workmen's cables dug in as they tried to pull the columns down.

Another temple completed by Antoninus is the Temple of Venus and Rome, which stands on the rising ground of the

Part of the shrine to Vesta.

Velia, between the Colosseum and the Forum. This was started by Hadrian, who fell out with his architect Apollodorus over its construction. Apollodorus complained that the *cella* was too small for its statue, and Hadrian, who had designed that part personally, was so offended that he had the architect killed. The temple's *cellae* are surrounded by a portico, with the goddess Roma's chamber facing the Forum, and Venus looking towards the

Colosseum. Talking of the Colosseum, the gigantic statue that gives the area its name had to be moved to allow the construction of this temple, and it took a team of 26 elephants to do the job.

Finally, at the Forum Boarium take a moment to admire the circular temple to Hercules (so like the shrine to Vesta it is sometimes mistaken for it), and the Temple of Portunus beside it. Rather in keeping with his macho image, the altar

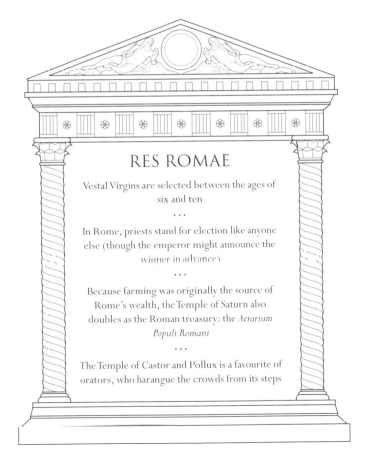

RES ROMAE

Vestal Virgins are selected between the ages of six and ten

, , ,

In Rome, priests stand for election like anyone else (though the emperor might announce the winner in advance)

, , ,

Because farming was originally the source of Rome's wealth, the Temple of Saturn also doubles as the Roman treasury: the *Aerarium Populi Romani*

, , ,

The Temple of Castor and Pollux is a favourite of orators, who harangue the crowds from its steps

outside Hercules' temple was for many years the largest in Rome, until Augustus built his altar of peace, the Ara Pacis (see Campus Martius p. 133).

This quick pilgrimage has skipped at least half a dozen other interesting temples, including that on the south-west of the Forum dedicated to the sons of Jupiter, Castor and Pollux, familiarly referred to as 'Castor's'. On the Aventine is the famous Temple of Diana but in the opposite direction, on the edge of the Campus Martius, is a temple which is among the greatest architectural wonders of Rome – the Pantheon.

THE PANTHEON

THE PANTHEON IS OVER THE RIVER from the massively imposing tomb of Hadrian, and near to the slightly smaller but still impressive mausoleum of Augustus and his family. The Pantheon can be seen from afar thanks to its massive dome, which requires walls 20 feet thick to support it. Yet despite its massive size, this dome is so exactly proportioned that if a gigantic perfect sphere were placed underneath it, the sphere would fit exactly, because the distance from the floor to the highest part of the dome is exactly equal to the dome's diameter, enclosing almost 2 million cubic feet of air.

The temple, including its dome, is the result of rebuilding by Hadrian in the early 2nd century AD. This temple is dedicated to all of the Olympian gods, each of whom has a statue set into its own niche in the walls (in Greek *pan* = all, *theon* = gods).

Entry is through massive bronze doors, behind a Greek-style frontage of granite columns, each 41 feet high and weighing 60 tons. Within, light streams through the 29-foot-wide circular opening at the top of the dome, creating a totally different atmosphere to the gloomier *cellae* of most gods; an atmosphere that changes as the sun moves through the day. Note how the concentric tiers of coffering which make up the dome have been partly hollowed out to reduce their weight, and how each

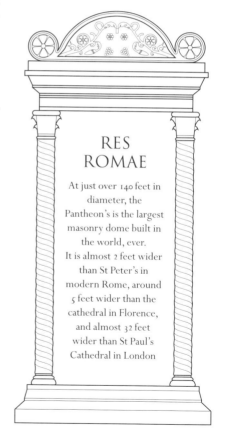

RES ROMAE

At just over 140 feet in diameter, the Pantheon's is the largest masonry dome built in the world, ever. It is almost 2 feet wider than St Peter's in modern Rome, around 5 feet wider than the cathedral in Florence, and almost 32 feet wider than St Paul's Cathedral in London

M. AGRIPPA L.F. COS.
TERTIUM FECIT
[MARCUS AGRIPPA, SON
OF LUCIUS, THREE TIMES
CONSUL, BUILT THIS]

THE ORIGINAL INSCRIPTION ON
THE PANTHEON, PRESERVED BY
HADRIAN FOR POSTERITY

tier becomes smaller to give a greater impression of size and space.

The rich marble flooring, the interarching columns and niches of the lower walls, the internal colonnades, and the profusion of light and colour combine to make this a temple of enduring fascination, an architectural and artistic *tour de force* that will endure for millennia.

RELIGIOUS FESTIVALS

MOST ROMAN HOMES OR HOSTELRIES have a calendar near the door, which are well worth consulting when making plans for the coming week. The markings in black and white are only of interest to the calendar's owner, and indicate lucky and unlucky days in his personal horoscope. Days marked F (*fastus*) and C (*comitialis*) in the calendar indicate working days and days when public assemblies may be held, and are basic weekdays. N is for *nefastus* and it means that some kinds of public business will not be carried out. EN is a half-and-half day in which public business is conducted only in the afternoon. NP, on the other hand, signals a complete shutdown and a major public holiday.

Some NP events, such as the Saturnalia, happen on fixed days, others are movable feasts in the style of the later celebration of Easter.

On the calendar, apart from the usual weekdays (often marked A H) and market days, are the three main divisions of the month – the start (the Kalends, sacred to Juno), the Nones (around the 7th) and on the 13th or 15th the Ides (sacred to Jupiter).

The Roman year is packed with festivals, many to gods no one remembers and whose rites are celebrated by priests in obscure temples. However, other celebrations are extremely public, and not only can a visitor not miss them, many visitors come to Rome especially for them.

January Bizarrely, 1 January is a normal working day, since the year used to begin in March, and the Romans don't change things more than necessary. But on this day the new consuls parade with their retinues up the Via Sacra to the Capitol, sacrifice white bulls to Jupiter for the safety of Rome, and are seated on ivory chairs as they are presented to the people. Early January also has the three-day festival of the Compitalia, a festival to pacify restless spirits. This includes plays, dances and sport. Slaves get the time off, so Roman citizens have to fend for themselves.

February This is the month of purification. During the week of the Parentalia, dead parents are remembered. Temples are closed, and no marriages take place. Little groups gather in cemeteries with jugs of wine and milk, sharing meals with the dead. The festival ends with all the family gathering for a huge family reunion and a slap-up meal. The Parentalia coincides with the Lupercalia, a rite so old that no one really understands the point of it. Two teams of aristocratic young men sacrifice goats and a dog in a small cave on the Palatine. Then, naked apart from the skins of the sacrificed goats, they race down the hill to the Forum, whipping anyone in their way with small strips of goatskin. Most of those in their path are young women, for the touch of the whips is supposed to guarantee fertility.

March Rituals in this month celebrate Mars after whom the month is named. A troupe of oddly dressed young men called *salii* go about the city, carrying strange shields and singing a hymn that even the Romans cannot understand. This rite is almost certainly older than Rome itself, and the youths are dressed in the antique bronze battle-gear of soldiers 1,000 years ago. As a reward for their chanting, they are rewarded every night with a meal so splendid that the phrase 'fit for the *salii'* now describes any particularly sumptuous repast.

April The month of blossoming (from Latin *aperio*, 'opening'). On 4 April there are banquets in honour of the Magna Mater (the Great Mother – an Asiatic cult). Then there is the Parilia, when a special mixture prepared by the Vestal Virgins is burned in small bonfires all over the city, and party-goers, after sprinkling themselves with water from a laurel branch, jump three times through the flames. Then everyone settles down to an open-air banquet. The Floralia is between 28 April and 3 May, a week of games and circuses dedicated to flowering and fertility. Sexual inhibitions are so lowered that not being able to get laid at the Floralia is almost a metaphor for unattractiveness or incompetence with the opposite sex.

May Worries about the spring harvest cause every farm and village to hold a 'lustration'. A procession goes around the village borders or around the crops, and rites are performed to Ceres. May is when a census of the Roman people may be carried out if the authorities feel one is required.

June 9 June is the Vestalia when married women are allowed into the forbidden parts of Vesta's shrine to make offerings. The month is unlucky until the Vestals have cleaned their sanctuary on the 15th, but despite this there is usually a drunken party held at the Temple of Minerva on the Ides of June. Then the whole population, including slaves and prisoners, sacrifices to Fortuna on 24 June. Everyone surges out of Rome to watch the ceremonies near the Vatican fields, and simultaneously tries out the new vintage of wine. On this day, Ovid remarks, there is no shame in rolling home drunk.

July The Apollonian Games from the 6th to the 13th have sporting, musical and theatrical events, but this is otherwise a quiet month.

VII Roman baths. These, the Thermae Antoninianae, better known as the Baths of Caracalla, are currently in the design stage on the architect's table, and work will begin in AD 212.

VIII The baths are not usually this empty, unless one arrives early or visits while the races are on. Instead, they tend to be aswarm with humanity shouting, splashing, lifting weights and buying unpalatable fast foods.

IX (*Overpage*) Temple *cella*. In Roman religion this is where the god lives. His worshippers sacrifice at his altar outside. The Romans are aware that the monumental statues within the *cellae* are not the gods themselves, but symbols of powerful abstract entities.

X View of the Pantheon interior. The Pantheon is one of the most impressive religious edifices ever constructed, and a worthy home for all the Olympian gods who are represented within.

XI (*Overpage*) View of the Pantheon, distorted to show the huge spherical space enclosed by the dome. Note the panels which make up the dome's interior, and how they are hollowed out to prevent their weight from becoming excessive.

August Many businessmen sacrifice to Hercules at the start of the month. The number of animals they sacrifice depends on their wealth, and no businessman likes to be thought poor. Because sacrifices to Hercules must be consumed at once within the temple precinct, there are many splendid free steak dinners to be had. The 13th is reserved for the cult of Diana on the Aventine, and is another day off for slaves. For some obscure reason women are supposed to wash their hair on this day. There is a festival to the ancient god Consus on 21 August, and this is interesting because chariot races used to take place around his temple. Now the site is the Circus Maximus, and the temple is right on the central barrier. The festival still takes place, but is followed by chariot racing.

September Only one festival: the games of the Ludi Romani which, lasting from the 5th to the 19th, crowd out all other events. On the Ides of September a nail is ceremonially driven into the walls of the Temple of Jupiter, and it is a popular occupation of tourists to count the nails in their serried rows. These now number more than 700.

October Has the festival of the October horse, which is a no-holds-barred horse race on the Campus Martius. Different

parts of the city can become violently partisan in their support of different horses. One of the winning horses is sacrificed, and its blood is used by the Vestal Virgins in one of their sacred festivals.

November Has the Plebeian Games, with a famous procession from the Capitol, through the Forum to the Circus. The Ides of November are for huge aristocratic banquets, and few dignitaries can be found out of town at this time. Who dines where and with whom establishes the social hierarchy for the coming year.

December Starts with the women-only festival to the Bona Dea (Good Goddess),

Sacrifice in progress outside a temple. Note that the officiating priest covers his head with part of his toga. Since the bull in the background looks a large one, it may be worth hanging around to see if there will be any large, meaty steaks on offer.

and finishes with the Saturnalia, which is launched with a huge public banquet in the Forum, open for everyone to attend. Shops are shut, presents are exchanged, there are games and parties and open gambling in the streets (usually forbidden by law). Formal clothing is discarded for party clothes, and people wear fancy hats on their heads. Every household chooses a master of ceremonies who dictates events, and on this one day the masters wait on their slaves.

RES ROMAE

February is named after the *februum*, an instrument of purification

, , ,

It is considered very unlucky to be married in May

, , ,

The 'lustration' will survive in Britain two millennia later, under the name of 'beating the bounds'

, , ,

On 1 April, women bathe in the public baths usually reserved for males, and pray to Fortuna Virilis for good luck with men

, , ,

A similar event to Rome's 'October horse' (though without the sacrifice) takes place at the *Palio* in 21st-century Siena, Italy

, , ,

The Rape of the Sabine women happened at the festival of Consus in the time of Romulus

MUST-SEE SITES

Forum of the Romans · Arch of Titus
Imperial Forums · Triumphal Columns
Tomb of St Peter · Baths

IX

S THE CAPITAL OF THE WORLD, ROME presents a different aspect to its many visitors. For some, Rome is an opportunity to meet the people who matter, be they in business or politics. For others the visit may be to the principal shrine of one of Rome's many gods. Others will be on government business, and many more will have come simply to see the fabled city for themselves. Each of these visitors will have their own ideas of what to do and see – but here are some that should be on the list of every newcomer to Rome.

FORUM OF THE ROMANS

I'll show you where you can easily find any kind of character, so that you can meet anyone you want without delay, be they vicious or virtuous, or decent or indecent.

PLAUTUS, *THE WEEVIL* 467

THE FORUM OF THE ROMANS SITS IN THE valley between the Palatine, Quirinal and Viminal hills, with the Esquiline at its base. Ever since the original boggy swamp between the hills was drained, this place has been so central to the life of the city that it is known simply as *the* Forum. It has changed since Plautus' day, and its importance has diminished somewhat since the end of the Republic, for many emperors have built additional forums to cope with the needs of the growing city. Nevertheless, the Forum of the Romans is still the place to go to meet friends, catch up on the latest gossip, watch impromptu entertainments from strolling players, or see top barristers pleading cases. For visitors, no trip to Rome is complete without a trip to the Forum, simply because so much of Rome's history happened in this one small valley. To stand before the senate house is to stand where Tarquin the Proud, Cincinnatus, Cato the Censor, Julius Caesar, Cicero, Nero and every other Roman of note has stood at some time in the last 800 years.

The Cloaca Maxima, Rome's great sewer, was the first major construction project in the Forum. In many ways it was the most important, for it drained the marshes which filled the valley and made building possible. That was in the time of the Etruscan kings and, ever since, the Forum has been a work in progress. The latest structure is the Arch of Septimius

Severus, still so new that the stone has not yet weathered.

This arch is on the site of the old Graecostasis, an area just outside the senate house where foreign embassies used to wait until they were summoned before the senate. This site, not coincidentally, gave ambassadors a splendid view of the Forum, Capitol and Palatine, and doubtless sent them to meet the senators with a proper and humble appreciation of the glories of Rome.

The Arch of Severus commemorates the emperor's victories in Asia over the Parthian empire. Its three vaults are completely sheathed in marble, the carvings showing carts laden with booty, the invincible armies of the empire, and a gigantic figure representing humbled Parthia herself. On top of the arch is a bronze sculpture of Septimius Severus on his triumphal chariot, flanked by riders on horseback. The inscription relates the deeds of the emperor, but finishes with the proud letters S.P.Q.R. – *Senatus Populusque Romanus*, 'The Senate and People of Rome'.

As you stand before the arch looking toward the Aventine hill, the Temple of Saturn is on the right, the Temple of Ves-

> *They [captured Carthaginian ships] were hauled to the docks in Rome and partly burned. It was agreed to decorate the raised platform in the Forum with their prows ('rostra'), and that space was called the Rostra*
>
> LIVY, *HISTORY OF ROME* 8.14

> *I remember [the lawyer Trachalus'] first appearance before a tribunal in the Julian Basilica. The usual four panels of judges were also in session, and the building was full of noise*
>
> QUINTILIAN, *INSTITUTIO ORATORIA* 10.1.119

pasian just behind that, and nearby is the ancient Temple of Concord. Built to embody the harmony of the social classes in Rome, the Temple of Concord is often neglected, and then ostentatiously restored and renovated after any social upheaval. A few paces away, just in front of the altar of Vulcan, is a little covered well. This is the *umbilicus urbis Romae*, literally the 'belly button of the city of Rome', and therefore the very centre of the entire empire of a fifth of the human race. (And as this area is a major tourist attraction, it sometimes seems as though much of that fifth of the human race is trying to share the Forum with you.)

On the left stands the Curia, Rome's senate house, with its imposing bronze doors. When the senate is meeting, a group of young men clusters about these doors with their tutors hovering nearby. These youngsters are the sons of senators, and it is their time-honoured privilege to stand listening to the debates, so that they are familiar with the senate's practices when they come to take their places on its marble benches.

The Rostra, after which every speaker's rostrum in the world is named, used to stand in front of the senate. Here speakers such as Cato the Censor used to harangue the Roman crowds, and here the heads of distinguished senators were displayed on pikes during the political strife and civil war of the early 1st century BC. The Rostra has now been moved to just in front of the Arch of Severus, between the altar of Vulcan and the Julian Basilica on the flanks of the Palatine hill.

Also right beside the new Arch of Severus is a small monument, so ancient that it is now partly underground. The Latin carved on this stubby pillar of black stone (*lapis niger*) is of an antiquity that makes it incomprehensible to modern Romans, but tradition has it that the spot marks the place where Rome's founder Romulus was taken up into heaven. (Or where he was murdered by senators who each concealed a bit of his corpse under their togas – there are two traditions explaining Romulus' mysterious disappearance.)

Join the pedestrians thronging the Via Sacra as they pass the *Lacus Curtius*, a bas-relief of a statue of a rider on horseback. Legend says that during the reign of the kings a gaping hole opened in the Forum, which was seen as an omen of doom. However, a young man named Curtius sacrificed himself and saved Rome by riding on his warhorse into the hole which closed up after him. Romans who know their history will quietly point out that more probably, if less dramatically, the site was fenced off by the consul Curtius in the 5th century BC after Jupiter claimed it as his own by repeatedly striking it with lightning. The people who like to hang around this area, says Plautus, are...

...impudent, spiteful windbags, who shamelessly slander others for no good reason, though there is a lot that could be said against those slanderers themselves, and in truth too.

PLAUTUS, *THE WEEVIL* 476

Drawing level with the equestrian statue of Domitian, it becomes plain that the Forum remains a vital administrative centre, with the courts noisily in session in the

View of the Palatine side of the Forum of the Romans, looking back towards the Capitoline.

Julian Basilica mostly behind to the left, and in the Aemilian Basilica coming up on the right.

Look at those milling about here, and decide if the words of Plautus are still true:

If you want a liar and a braggart, go to the temple of Cloacina [in front of the Aemilian Basilica]; for wealthy, spendthrift husbands, take a look around the Basilica. You'll also see worn-out whores and the men who still try, out of habit, to beat their prices down further.

PLAUTUS, *THE WEEVIL* 470

At the intersection leading to the Vicus Tuscus, a road runs towards the imperial residences on the Palatine, past the Temple of Castor and Pollux. ('Go behind the Temple of Castor, and you will run into those who can be trusted to quickly put you out of your misery,' warns Plautus.)

The Regia, home of Rome's *Pontifex Maximus* during the Republican era, is at this intersection. This building was once occupied by Julius Caesar. The *Pontifex Maximus* is the supervisor of the Vestal Virgins, whose temple and living quarters lie just beyond the Regia on the Palatine side. On the left stand two other temples, the Temple of Antoninus and Faustina, and a

Coin showing Temple of Venus and Rome.

smaller Temple of Romulus, which lies among some tombs which predate the founding of his city.

Ahead the ground rises away from the Forum area, and the view is dominated by the imposing Temple of Venus and Rome with the Colosseum looming beyond that.

ARCH OF TITUS

THE ARCH OF TITUS LIES BETWEEN THE Forum and the Colosseum, and the passage beneath the arch is packed with people moving between the two. Still, it is worth standing against this human tide to admire one of the most imposing of the two dozen or so triumphal arches scattered about the city. Triumphal arches are a particularly Roman form of architecture, and each commemorates a military victory of particular splendour. The Arch of Titus commemorates the defeat of the Judean revolt in AD 70.

Titus commanded only the latter part of this campaign, for his father Vespasian left the job to him while he conquered the rest of the Roman empire, which had been in chaos since the death of Nero. The arch partly celebrates Titus' relief at a successful first command, and partly commemorates his memory, having been completed after Titus' death by his brother Domitian. Within the arch bas-reliefs depict the booty displayed in Titus' triumphal procession, including the seven-branched candelabrum and silver trumpets from the Temple of Jerusalem. In the facing scene Titus rides his triumphal chariot, while Winged Victory crowns him with a wreath, and Roma, dressed as an Amazon, leads the horses. The reliefs and the floral pattern of the top interior of the arch are vividly painted and partly gilded, and seem almost to move with the play of sunshine and shadow on the sculpture.

Titus had his monument carefully positioned so that the approaching crowds can see the Curia and main buildings of the Forum framed within the arch, the power of the emperors encompassing the majesty of the Republic.

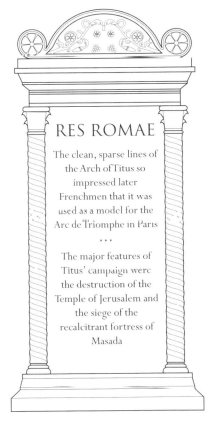

RES ROMAE

The clean, sparse lines of the Arch of Titus so impressed later Frenchmen that it was used as a model for the Arc de Triomphe in Paris

. . .

The major features of Titus' campaign were the destruction of the Temple of Jerusalem and the siege of the recalcitrant fortress of Masada

THE SENATE AND PEOPLE OF ROME HAVE DEDICATED THIS ARCH TO THE DEIFIED TITUS VESPASIAN AUGUSTUS, THE SON OF THE DEIFIED VESPASIAN

CAPTION ON THE ARCH OF TITUS

IMPERIAL FORUMS

SINCE THE TIME OF JULIUS CAESAR, NO emperor seems able to rule the city without depositing a forum somewhere within it. These forums form a dense block between the Quirinal and Viminal hills on the one side, and the Forum of the Romans on the other.

Caesar's contribution, started in the late 50s BC, cost a fortune before any stones were laid, since before building Caesar had to buy and demolish 14,000 square yards of very highly priced private residences. A colonnade runs around the elongated rectangular forum, which is dominated by Caesar's Temple to Venus Genetrix at one end. This was Caesar's unsubtle reminder that his family claimed divine ancestry through Venus, mother of Aeneas, and the grandmother of Iulus. Beneath the magnif-

Here, where the forums are now, was a deep swamp, a ditch dripping with water washed back from the river

OVID, *FASTI* 6.401–2

icently decorated temple ceiling the aesthetes browse through Caesar's splendid art collection, a reflection of his impeccable taste.

There is a fine marble statue of the dictator in military uniform, and a gilded statue of Caesar's old flame Cleopatra of Egypt. In fact, the statue of Cleopatra shows a lady with Greek features and a large nose – Cleopatra's charms were more than physical.

Perhaps the best thing about this forum is the fountain. On hot summer days visitors lounge downwind in its cooling spray and admire the neo-Attic curves of the lightly dressed nymphs which decorate it.

Caesar built the Temple of Venus Genetrix, as he had vowed to do before the battle of Pharsalus ... by the side of the goddess he put a beautiful statue of Cleopatra, which stands there to this day

APPIAN, *CIVIL WARS* 2.102

and the firewall also blocks out some of the hubbub from that populous precinct.) Secondly, this forum is not quite rectangular. The owner of one of the houses on the corner refused to sell, and Augustus, keen to reinforce the idea of Republican normality, decided not to confiscate the offending property.

Often there is a small crowd gawking at Julius Caesar's sword, which is on display in this forum. And among the numerous statues and works of art are two paintings by Apelles, one of the great artists of antiquity.

CAESAR'S TEMPLE WAS TO VENUS, but that of Augustus, his adopted son, was to Mars Ultor – Mars the Avenger. Augustus' patron god was Apollo (there is an ivory statue to Apollo in this forum as well), but Augustus wanted to emphasize that he had avenged Caesar's assassination while incidentally seizing supreme power for himself.

The temple priests point out two interesting features of this forum. One is that Augustus protected the temple and much of the Forum of the Romans with a large firewall on the Subura side. (Augustus' forum lies between Caesar's forum and the Subura,

Should we not mention among our noble buildings ... the Forum of Augustus?

PLINY, *NATURAL HISTORY* 36.102

VESPASIAN'S, THE MOST EASTERLY forum, lies very close to the Via Sacra. It is sometimes called the Forum of Peace, since a large temple to Peace dominates the site. This forum is particularly interesting for Jewish historians since the temple is a museum packed with treasures and artifacts looted from Judea after the rebellion in AD 70.

Nerva's forum would have been Domitian's if that unpopular emperor had not been assassinated before it was finished. Domitian's successor was not prepared to risk the wrath of Minerva by changing the temple of Domitian's favourite deity, so the temple remains, a fine building in the Corinthian style. Its serenity is completely spoiled by the traffic streaming from the Quirinal hill to the Forum of the Romans, since the main road between the two runs right across the forecourt.

The foot of the Quirinal also hosts the most northerly and the grandest and busiest of all the imperial forums. Trajan's forum was designed by his favourite architect, Apollodorus (see previous chapter for this poor man's fate at the hands of Hadrian), who created the huge (980 by 280 feet) administrative and commercial centre by cutting deep into the slope of the Quirinal. The forum is partly a market serving the needs of the bustling nearby Subura (see **Shopping** p. 63), partly a law court, and partly a library. The multi-storey library buildings are a state archive, second only to the Tabularium in importance, and a cool, quiet refuge from the bustle of the forum below. One library building contains Greek documents, the other Latin. The books and scrolls are carefully preserved in wooden presses in

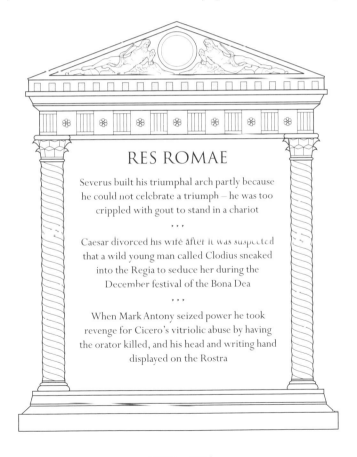

RES ROMAE

Severus built his triumphal arch partly because he could not celebrate a triumph – he was too crippled with gout to stand in a chariot

, , ,

Caesar divorced his wife after it was suspected that a wild young man called Clodius sneaked into the Regia to seduce her during the December festival of the Bona Dea

, , ,

When Mark Antony seized power he took revenge for Cicero's vitriolic abuse by having the orator killed, and his head and writing hand displayed on the Rostra

recesses in the walls. Beyond the libraries stands a massive temple to Trajan, its grandeur emphasizing the ever-increasing power and resources of the empire.

TRIUMPHAL COLUMNS

TRAJAN'S COLUMN. TRAJAN'S FORUM IS dominated by this huge column. Pause respectfully before joining the tourists at the stone plinth upon which it rests, for it is in fact a funerary marker – Trajan's ashes lie in a small chamber on the north side of the base, just as his statue tops off the structure. (This statue will go absent without leave during the Middle Ages and be replaced by one of St Peter.)

A 200-metre frieze spirals up the column, telling the story of Trajan's Dacian wars. The design represents an unrolled scroll, a reference to the column's position between the Greek and Roman libraries. Even if they have no interest in Greek and Roman texts, some tourists visit the libraries just to admire the sculptures on the column from the upper floors. The sculptures are a pictorial counterpoint to Trajan's written account of the wars (sadly lost to later ages). The gap between the wars (AD 101–102 and 105–106) is indicated by the figure of Victory writing on a shield. Trajan appears 60 times, conducting sieges and negotiations, battles, river crossings and cavalry actions, in a series of vignettes that tell more about the Roman army at war than any other single monument in antiquity.

And in his forum [Trajan] set up a great column, both for his own burial place, and to show the scale of his works in building the forum. For all that ground was hilly, but he excavated it to a depth equal to the height of the column

CASSIUS DIO, *ROMAN HISTORY* 68.16

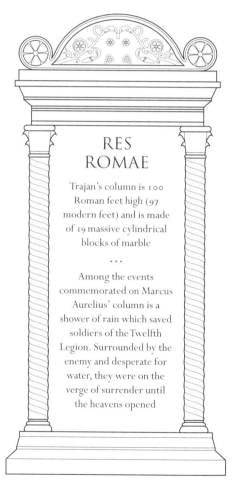

RES ROMAE

Trajan's column is 100 Roman feet high (97 modern feet) and is made of 19 massive cylindrical blocks of marble

. . .

Among the events commemorated on Marcus Aurelius' column is a shower of rain which saved soldiers of the Twelfth Legion. Surrounded by the enemy and desperate for water, they were on the verge of surrender until the heavens opened

Coin showing Trajan's column.

M ARCUS AURELIUS' COLUMN. A BRISK 15-minute walk northward from the Capitoline hill, passing the Pantheon on the left, brings you to an imitation of Trajan's column which is well worth a visit in its own right. This column, a memorial to the philosopher-emperor Marcus Aurelius, was erected in about AD 190.

Romans assert that Marcus Aurelius was one of Rome's best emperors, just as his recently assassinated and deeply unloved son Commodus was among the worst. The column, actually built by Commodus, commemorates Marcus Aurelius' wars against the Germans and Sarmatians (the latter a tribe of warrior horsemen in the Black Sea region). As with Trajan's column, a relief of Victory writing on a shield divides the narrative into two parts.

Round off a visit to the column by looking at the house of Adrastus, the caretaker of this monument. The inscription written at the column's base testifies he was given permission to construct his house from the timber originally used as scaffolding while the column was being raised.

The column shows three emperors – Marcus Aurelius, the current emperor, his son Commodus who succeeds him, and Pertinax, the general who succeeds Commodus.

TOMB OF ST PETER

T HE VATICAN HILL, LYING ON THE north-east of Rome, is a rather boggy and gloomy place, believed to be a haunt of witches, and primarily used by workers who dig the hill's clay and burn it into bricks. To reach the site, go from the city towards the Circus of Nero. This circus was started by Gaius Caligula and used by Nero for private practice at his hobby of chariot racing. It was only briefly opened to the public after the Great Fire of Rome, and is now disused.

Nero opened his circus not for chariot racing, but for the public execution of Christians blamed for the conflagration which destroyed much of Rome. The historian Tacitus says that some of the Christians were covered with animal skins so that savage dogs would tear them to pieces; others were smeared with tar and candle wax, then burned at the stake; others were crucified. Among those crucified here two years later was the leader of the Christian church in Rome, St Peter. Tradition says that the Apostle was executed *inter duas metas* – that is, on the central barrier of the race track. If so, he died beside the obelisk that was later moved a few hundred yards from the circus to stand ever after in front of the great basilica that grew over the saint's tomb.

The *Liber Pontificalis,* a book based on the earliest Christian traditions, says that Peter was buried 'near the Circus of Nero, between the Via Aurelia and the Via Triumphalis, near the place where he was crucified'. Peter's grave was either on land owned by a Christian, or being just over the road from the circus, was already used for disposal of the dead. The Romans seldom disturb the tombs of the dead, whosoever they were while alive, so Peter's burial place has never been a secret. In fact, it became a place of pilgrimage almost from the day it was dug.

The saint's body lies in a sarcophagus in a small underground vault, and the area has become crowded with the graves of those wishing to be buried as close as possible nearby. At this time, the burial site is called the Tropaion of St Peter. Considering the future consequence of the religion he brought to Rome, Peter's tomb is rather humble and inconspicuous. A gabled roof covers the graves, and the wall enclosing one side is instantly recognizable as it is painted bright red. To the annoyance of the devout caretakers of the tomb, the wall often bears graffiti asking for Peter's intercession, though it is uncertain how defacing his resting place will put the saint into an amenable frame of mind.

BATHS

ONE UNMATCHED BENEFIT OF ROMAN civilization is the public baths. Among the first signs that a legionary camp has become permanent is the presence of a bath house, and towards the centre of civilization, the baths become larger and grander, with the best to be found in Rome itself. All the baths have a changing room (*apodyterium*) heated by warm air, a warm bath (*tepidarium*), a hot room with hot air and hot baths (*caldarium*), and a room with a refreshing cold plunge bath (*frigidarium*). Romans don't just go to the baths to wash. They might spend an entire afternoon enjoying the facilities, gossiping with old friends and making new ones. The philosopher Seneca gives some idea of what is on offer, though he was not entirely enthusiastic about living so close to these social centres.

RES ROMAE

Early Christians buried their sacred dead as near as possible to where they were martyred, resulting in many burials being extremely close to the Circus of Nero

. . .

Among those who lie with the first bishop of Rome is Linus, his successor

The hubbub makes you sorry that you are not deaf. I hear the beefcake boys wheezing and grunting as they lift their lead weights, and the masseur's hands slapping their shoulders. Then, the ball players arrive and start yelling out the score — that's usually all I can take. But there's also those people who plunge themselves into the water with an almighty splash, and that only gives a mild idea of what goes on. At least these people have normal voices. Apart from them there is the depilator who screeches for customers and never shuts up until he's stripping the hair from someone's armpits and making them yell even louder than he does. Then there's the drinks pedlar, and the sausage salesman, and all the other hucksters, each bawling in his own special way

SENECA, *LETTERS TO LUCILIUS* 56

To honour these noble institutions, we recommend a tour of Rome's baths in chronological order.

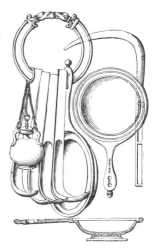

Bathing implements.

THE BATHS OF AGRIPPA. STANDING IN the Campus Martius, these baths are the oldest public baths in Rome. They were started in 25 BC but had to wait for the completion of the Aqua Virgo aqueduct in 19 BC to be fully functional. They are near another building commissioned by Agrippa, the Pantheon, and like the Pantheon, they have been extensively remodelled by Hadrian. The baths are smaller than later versions (though still covering about 10,700 square feet) and lack many of the later amenities. The plan is rather similar to the much larger and later baths in Trèves (Trier). The hot room has a fresco which is worth seeing, and there are numerous works of art throughout, including paintings and a well-known statue, the Apoxyomenos of Lysippus. These baths can get crowded, since being nearest to the Campus Martius, they are the first port of call for those boisterous souls who have just been exercising, playing sport or horse-riding in the fields.

THE BATHS OF NERO. 'AHH … WHAT could be worse than Nero, or better than his baths?' sighed the poet Martial after a relaxing afternoon at this amenity. These baths, the aesthete's favourite, were built in the last decade of Nero's reign, near to the baths of Agrippa, making the folk of this area the cleanest in Rome. Nero's architect made some changes to Agrippa's design so that the *frigidarium* is in the middle of the north side, and the *tepidarium* between it and the *caldarium*. The baths are architecturally splendid and magnificently adorned. Strolling through large colonnaded courts on the east and west sides of the central hall, a visitor can choose between the four dressing and lounging rooms on each side of the *caldarium*. There is an indoor gymnasium (the first permanent building of this kind in Rome) for those who want to work up a sweat even when the weather is bad. Nero's ideas were adopted by later designers, giving the baths their present role as the leisure centres of Rome.

THE BATHS OF TITUS. THESE BATHS TOO were contributed by Nero, albeit indirectly, since the emperor Titus had them constructed from Nero's magnificent Golden House, decommissioned after the tyrant's fall. Completed in AD 81, the baths stand near the Colosseum and cost one *as* for entry. Smaller than the other baths, these are particularly appreciated by aficionados of Neronian decadence.

THE BATHS OF TRAJAN. THESE ARE THE work of Apollodorus, the designer of Trajan's forum. In AD 104, after a fire on the Esquiline hill, Trajan decided that the water supply designated by Nero for his private use could be better used for public baths. As with all of Trajan's projects, this was on a massive scale. The baths are set in their own gardens and surrounded by sports facilities and libraries. *Mens sana in corpore sano* ('a healthy mind in a healthy body') indeed!

RES ROMAE

Trajan's baths extend over 1,076,426 square feet and are sometimes occupied by over 1,000 people at once. The main cistern can hold a massive 2 million gallons of water

Those who have studied the customs of our early history tell us that people washed arms and legs every day ... but washed the whole body only three times a month

SENECA, *LETTERS TO LUCILIUS* 86

ROMAN WALKS

The Palatine · Along the Tiber
The Campus Martius

X

WALKING IN ROME IS NOT AN unadulterated pleasure, because many others are doing the same. At the wrong time of day the main thoroughfares are packed, and you venture into the side streets at your peril.

The crossing of waggons in the narrow winding streets, the cursing competitions of drovers when brought to a standstill ... however we might try to hurry, we are blocked by a surging crowd in front, and by a dense mass of people pressing in on us from behind. One man digs me with his elbow, another prods me with the hard pole of a sedan chair. Someone bangs a plank against my head and someone else follows that up with a wine-cask. My legs are smeared with mud [and if you are lucky, it will be mud]; soon huge feet trample all over me, and a soldier lands his hobnailed boot solidly on my toe.

JUVENAL, *SATIRES* 3.236–7; 243–8

However, choose a quiet time of day, when the brick is honey-brown in the sunlight, and pigeons cluster on the red-tiled roofs, and Rome can be a magical place.

THE PALATINE

THE FIRST WALK GOES PAST SOME buildings still under construction and others dating back to the legendary origins of Rome. Because the Palatine is the home of the emperor himself, expect to be stopped several times by suspicious guards and have a *very* good explanation for being there. You might claim religious devotion since the Palatine is home to many temples; in fact some cult sites on this hill were ancient before Romulus and Remus were born.

Start on the northern slopes of the Palatine with the Arch of Titus at your back, walking up an ancient road called the Clivus Palatinus. The road will be thronged with courtiers and petitioners to the imperial court, together with merchants seeking contracts and local tradesmen who already supply the palace. The first stop is the Cryptoporticus of Nero. A cryptoporticus is a gallery which, being semi-underground, remains cool even in midsummer. The tyrant emperor's gallery was lavishly decorated in stucco and allowed him to stroll in comfort down the hill to his magnificent Golden House (now demolished to make way for the Colosseum). At the Cryptoporticus, turn towards the first of the great imperial palaces of the Palatine, the Domus Tiberiana, which covers much of the west side of the hill. Gaius Caligula extended it so far that parts reached the Forum near the Temple of Castor and Pollux.

Beyond the Domus Tiberiana is the Temple of Magna Mater (the Great Mother), the route to which goes past the very oldest part of Rome, the hut of Romulus himself. This crude hut, with its thatched roof and mud walls, may seem totally artificial amid the imperial splendour, but later archaeological excavations will reveal that there was indeed a settlement here in the 8th century BC when Romulus is said to have lived on the Palatine with his wife Hersilia.

The Temple of Magna Mater stands on a lofty podium in a grove of oak trees. The goddess, in the form of a large black stone (possibly a meteorite), was brought to Rome from the East in 204 BC, in the midst of the war against Hannibal. During the Megalesian Games, which are dedicated to the goddess, theatrical and athletic events take place on the platform opposite. The Romans are both fascinated and repulsed by the *galli,* the goddesses' castrated devotees who wear feminine robes and jewelry. Worship of the goddess is said to bring ecstatic delight and insensitivity to pain

Caligula would often sit between the brother gods [Castor and Pollux], whose temple he had turned into the forecourt of his own house, and there he would offer himself for the adoration of visitors to the temple

SUETONIUS, *CALIGULA* 22

(which must help during the castration process).

On the central part of the hill is the Domus Augustana, once home to the emperor Augustus. Before Augustus, the Palatine housed many elite Roman households. Cicero lived here, as did Mark Antony, and the emperor Tiberius was born on this hill in 42 BC. But the Palatine was gradually taken over by Augustus' ever-expanding palace and temples such as that to Apollo, resplendent in gleaming white marble with doors of gold and ivory, its inner room packed with treasure and priceless statuary, such as the Diana of Timotheus and the magnificent Apollo of Skopas. This temple is closely integrated with Augustus' palace. In fact from the emperor's private study, to where he was fond of withdrawing, there is a good view of both the temple and the Circus Maximus.

His palace was considerably remodelled by Domitian, who was so unpopular that he had highly polished stone mirrors placed on the columns of the porticoes to spot assassins creeping up behind him. (Which did not help – he was assassinated in AD 96.) Just beyond Augustus' house is the separate residence of his wife Livia. Some beautiful frescoes, said to be from this house, survive in Roman museums 2,000 years later.

More modern parts of the imperial

complex are on the west of the hill; colonnades with fountains splashing in the centre, small gardens tended by industrious slaves, marble hallways decorated with priceless statues, and smaller buildings with brickwork covered with frescoes showing seascapes and mythological scenes. Palace officials scurry about with clay tablets and papyrus scrolls, elegantly dressed aristocrats in muttering coteries snootily regard nervous petitioners waiting to be called into the imperial presence.

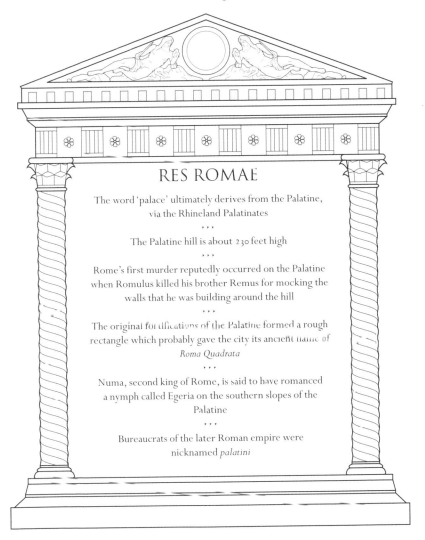

RES ROMAE

The word 'palace' ultimately derives from the Palatine, via the Rhineland Palatinates

...

The Palatine hill is about 230 feet high

...

Rome's first murder reputedly occurred on the Palatine when Romulus killed his brother Remus for mocking the walls that he was building around the hill

...

The original fortifications of the Palatine formed a rough rectangle which probably gave the city its ancient name of *Roma Quadrata*

...

Numa, second king of Rome, is said to have romanced a nymph called Egeria on the southern slopes of the Palatine

...

Bureaucrats of the later Roman empire were nicknamed *palatini*

These petitioners meet their god and emperor in a basilica lined with colossal statues and dominated by the emperor's raised throne at one end. Those more intimate with the emperor meet him in the imperial council chambers (also in this basilica), or dine with him in the state triclinium, the *coenatio Iovis*.

From the palace the walk leads to a wide peristyle and a small temple dedicated by Domitian to his patron goddess Minerva. It passes beside a long wall which protects an elegant and unusually secure garden where the emperor can relax in relative privacy. (It is probably here, in later years, that the Syrian emperor Elagabalus will take his rather unusual pleasures.)

[Elagabalus] harnessed very beautiful women to a little one-wheeled carriage … and would drive about like this naked, and they were naked as they pulled him

ANON, *HIST. AUG. ELAGABALUS*
29.2

For now, the walk has to detour eastwards to avoid work on a huge artificial platform overlooking the Circus Maximus which is being built so that the emperor can enjoy the excitement of the races without leaving home.

There is still more construction downhill where the Baths of Livia are being augmented and further baths added. The walk finishes beneath the arches of the Aqua Claudia, having completed the greater part of a large circle. The Colosseum is now on the left, and the Circus Maximus behind to the right. It is a short walk to the Forum Boarium where the walk along the Tiber begins.

ALONG THE TIBER

START IN THE THRONGED MARKET OF the Forum Boarium beside the bronze bull which would tell you, if the noise and smell had not already done so, that this is Rome's main cattle market. It lies between the Forum and the Clivus Publicus, the main road from the Aventine hill, and also takes traffic from the south of the Palatine and the valley of the Circus Maximus, so the crowds are often dense. On the river edge of the market a quadrangular seawall encloses the docks of the Emporium where barges from Ostia are unloaded. A crowd of idlers and cutpurses looks over the new arrivals, while longshoremen hang about for commissions to unload the barges into the warehouses that lie between the Forum and the Aventine. While moving through the market, keep an eye on those cattle with hay tied on their horns, for this indicates a particularly dangerous beast.

At the upstream end of the market is the Sublician bridge, the oldest of the bridges of Rome. Here Horatius is said to have held out heroically against the Etruscan soldiers of king Tarquin who tried to destroy Rome's nascent Republic. Rome's priests are called Pontifices (pontiffs) because of their connection with this bridge, any damage to which is seen as a sign from the gods. The bridge is completely of wood without iron or stone, now as a matter of tradition, but originally because, when it was Rome's only bridge, the wooden framework made it easier to pull down in the face of an advancing enemy. These days the wooden piles (*sublicae*) which gave the bridge its name have been replaced by firmer stone foundations.

After crossing the river, turn right and walk along the Tiber. The river is reaching the end of its 250-mile journey to the sea, a journey which started in the Apennine hills, then past the city of Narnia into the plain of Latium. The river has now slowed sufficiently to drop some of the silt which gives it a colour which the Romans call Tiber Yellow, and it twists snakelike through the city. A line of stones (*cippi*, as used for the *pomerium*) marks the limits of the authority of the commissioners who control the banks and ensure the smooth flow of the river – not always successfully.

The west bank is the unfashionable side, and when the wind is in the wrong direction it carries the stench of the tanneries which are banned from more prestigious parts of town. The Tiber itself can smell pretty ripe too, since the Romans discharge or dump much of their sewage into 'Father Tiber' and let it carry dead dogs, rubbish and the occasional human corpse out of the city.

We have seen the tawny Tiber, his waves flung back from the Etruscan shore, go to the left [east] bank and overthrow the regal monuments and the Temple of Vesta

HORACE, *ODES* 1.2.13–16

I am he whom you see, cleaving these banks and cutting through rich farmland in full flow – the Tiber of the blue waters, the most beloved river of heaven

VERGIL, *AENEID* 8.62–64

Despite this, the Romans are not averse to an occasional dip in the river (presumably the further upstream the better!). This attracts a certain amount of interest, since public nudity is rare in Rome. Cicero remarked to one lady:

You have gardens on the Tiber. You deliberately selected that particular site because they are at the very place where all the young men go swimming.

CICERO, *PRO CAELIO* 15 (36)

Return to the east bank of the river over the Aemilian bridge, the oldest stone bridge in the city, built in about 142 BC. The bridge was restored by Augustus, and it is probably his handiwork which will survive into 20th-century Rome as a lonely arch in the middle of the river.

Just before the next bridge, a few hundred yards upstream, is the Theatre of Marcellus, dedicated by Augustus in about 17 BC to the memory of his recently deceased nephew of that name. With walls over 98 feet high, and seating over 14,000 spectators, this is the grandest of Rome's stone theatres. On the walls of the first floor, between each arch, one mask is carved, each a representative of the stylized theatrical repertoire: ten from comedy, five from tragedy, and five from satyr plays.

The Theatre of Marcellus is now only a few centuries into its journey through the millennia in which it will become a fortress, a noble house, and finally a set of residential apartments.

Turning back to the river, cross over the Fabrician bridge to the Tiber island. The Romans claim that their ancestors, want-

The emperor Claudius, distressed that 'certain men were exposing their sick and worn-out slaves on the Island of Aesculapius [Tiber Island] because of the trouble of treating them', decreed all such slaves were to be free men, even if they recovered

SUETONIUS, *CLAUDIUS* 25

ing nothing to do with King Tarquin after his overthrow, hurled the grain from his fields into the Tiber, where silt accumulated about it until the island was formed. In reality, this is where the river divides to flow around a rocky spur of the Capitoline hill. For many years this island was considered cursed, and suitable only for social outcasts. Then the Romans brought a statue of the god of healing, Aesculapius, to their city in 292 BC. As the attendants on the ship carrying the god's sacred snake prepared for their arrival, the snake escaped over the side. It swam to the island, and there the god's temple was built in deference to his obvious intention.

Other temples were added, and now shares the island's 820-foot length with Jupiter, Faunus, and the personification of the Tiber itself. To commemorate the snake's aquatic adventure, the island has been made into roughly the shape of a ship, forever sailing downstream with Aesculapius' temple at the bows. This temple is crowded, for it is the nearest Rome has to a hospital (and there will be one on the island ever afterwards).

There is a good view from the island, because the Romans leave the riverside

RES ROMAE

It was the fate of a condemned criminal to have his body dragged through the streets on a hook and then hurled into the Tiber

. . .

Ostia, the grain port of Rome, lies another 16 miles downstream from Rome

. . .

The Aelian bridge will later be called the Bridge of the Angels after the statues of the Renaissance architect and sculptor Bernini which decorate it

The mausoleum of Augustus.

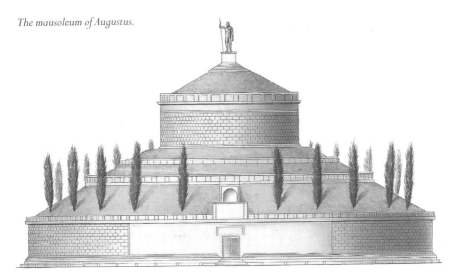

free for wharves which load and unload a never-ending stream of barges from dawn well into the night.

Leave the island by the Cestian bridge (built in the 60s BC at the same time as the Fabrician on the opposite bank) and go upstream to where the emperor Hadrian lies buried in Rome's biggest tomb.

It is a most notable sight, made of Parian marble with the stones fitted together so closely that no joints are visible. It has four equal sides, each a stone's throw (300 feet) in length, and of a height greater than the city wall. Above, there are statues of men and horses, of the same marble and superbly crafted.

PROCOPIUS, *THE GOTHIC WAR* 1.32

At the top is a massive statue of the emperor riding a four-horse chariot. Before Hadrian, Rome's emperors were generally buried in the mausoleum of

Augustus, but this had no more room. So unless Rome was to fill up with imperial burial markers such as Trajan's column, another repository for imperial corpses had to be found, and Hadrian's mausoleum (built in AD 134) has room enough for another century's worth of emperors.

Leave the tomb by the Aelian bridge which connects Hadrian's memorial with the city. Ahead lies the final Roman walk to the Pantheon and the Campus Martius.

THE CAMPUS MARTIUS

IN ADDITION TO ITS NATURAL BEAUTY, the Campus Martius has been made yet more attractive by careful planning. The size of the Campus is truly remarkable. There is space not only for the chariot-races and all kinds of other equestrian exercises, but also for the crowds of people who exercise by ball-playing, hoop-trundling and wrestling; and they can all do this at the same time without getting in each other's way. The works of art dotted around the field, the ground (which is grassy throughout the year), and the tops of the hills that loom over the river and stretch down to the banks, all make it look like a stage backdrop – a spectacle that you can hardly take your eyes off. And near this there is another area enclosed with numerous colonnades, and sacred precincts, and three theatres, and an amphitheatre, and magnificently furnished temples, one after another, so close together that they seem to be trying to make the rest of the city seem a mere suburb.

Because they believe that this is the holiest place of all, here the Romans have chosen to place the tombs of their most illustrious men and women. The most noteworthy is called the mausoleum of Augustus. This is a great mound near the river on a high foundation of white marble, thickly covered with evergreen trees, with a bronze image of Augustus Caesar at the very top. Beneath are the tombs of Augustus, his friends and his family, and behind the mound is a large sacred precinct with wonderful promenades.

The Campus Martius (which most Romans call simply 'the Campus') lies mostly between the Quirinal hill and the Tiber in the direction of the Vatican fields. As Strabo says, it is an ideal escape from the noise and crowds of the city, even if buildings and monuments have restricted the open space considerably in recent years.

It is believed that these fields were once owned by the kings of Rome, and on their expulsion the new Republic dedicated the land to Mars. It was an appropriate choice of deity, for even now young men practise horse-riding, being taken carefully by their instructors through the manoeuvres they will soon be executing as cavalrymen of Rome. It was in these fields that the aged general Marius caused great embarrassment by rehearsing military exercises in the hope of commanding another army, though he was considered far too old for the job. In the days of the Republic this was also where the Roman people gathered to elect their senior magistrates and to vote on issues of peace or war. Here the Romans met ambassadors who were not entitled to enter the city since the Campus lies beyond the *pomerium*.

Start at the Theatre of Pompey, built by Julius Caesar's great rival in 55 BC. Spend an hour or two among the gardens and colonnades of the theatre, and admire the temple at the top which made it possible. At the time it was built, stone theatres were forbidden in Rome, so Pompey's architect made the stone benches of the theatre ostensibly steps leading to the temple (see plates IV and V). This little temple has the grandest staircase in the world, since over 10,000 people can sit on the 'steps' to watch a performance on the stage below.

If time permits, look at the Circus Flaminius, at the southern end of the Campus. Otherwise, wander among the many temples scattered through this area. As well as a temple to Mars, and an even older one to Bellona, the ancient goddess of war, you can find temples to the many exotic gods of the different peoples of the empire, which Roman piety does not permit within the city itself.

This perambulation should finish at the twin pillars of bronze before the mausoleum of Augustus. On these pillars Augustus had inscribed his *Res Gestae,* an account of his life and achievements, carefully edited to show Rome's first emperor in the best possible light. The tomb has an Egyptian look, since Augustus commissioned it in 29 BC, soon after conquering Egypt and visiting the tomb of Alexander the Great. Many later emperors are also buried in Augustus' mausoleum, including Vespasian, whose death was foretold by a fissure appearing in its walls.

To the north there is another grand obelisk which is in fact the pointer of a giant sundial. This too was designed by Augustus, and on his birthday, the shadow of the obelisk points directly at the Ara Pacis, Augustus' altar of peace, one of the finest examples of Roman sculpture ever created.

The altar dates from 9 BC. It is enclosed by walls of white marble on which are carved bas-reliefs of garlands and flowers. Above this are reliefs of the imperial family, the priests, senators and Roman people going in procession to give thanks for the blessings of the Roman peace. The portraits combine the effortless elegance of Greek sculpture with a grandeur fitting to an imperial city. Not by coincidence, this complex lies alongside the Via Flaminia.

Those entering or leaving the city by that great highway are greeted or sent on their way by this evocative memorial, a symbol of all that is splendid in the capital of the world, the Rome of the Caesars.

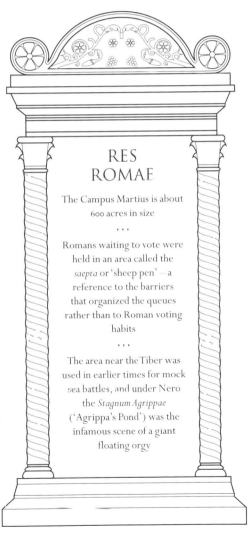

RES ROMAE

The Campus Martius is about 600 acres in size

· · ·

Romans waiting to vote were held in an area called the *saepta* or 'sheep pen' – a reference to the barriers that organized the queues rather than to Roman voting habits

· · ·

The area near the Tiber was used in earlier times for mock sea battles, and under Nero the *Stagnum Agrippae* ('Agrippa's Pond') was the infamous scene of a giant floating orgy

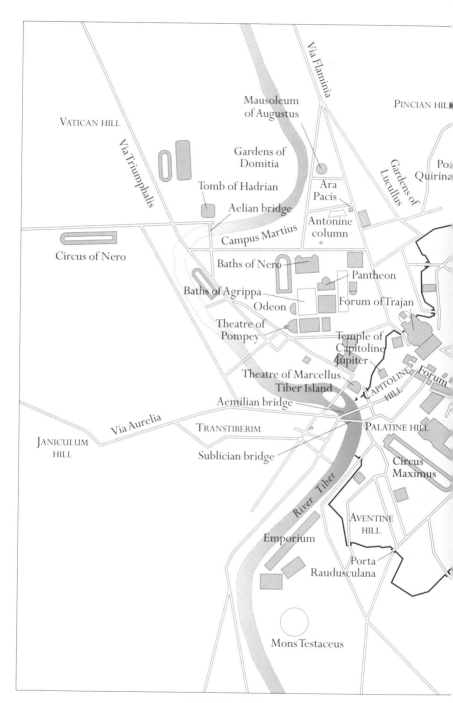

VATICAN HILL

Via Triumphalis

Circus of Nero

Via Flaminia

Mausoleum of Augustus

PINCIAN HILL

Gardens of Domitia

Tomb of Hadrian

Aelian bridge

Ara Pacis

Antonine column

Gardens of Lucullus

Po... Quirina...

Campus Martius

Baths of Nero

Baths of Agrippa

Odeon

Theatre of Pompey

Pantheon

Forum of Trajan

Temple of Capitoline Jupiter

Theatre of Marcellus

Tiber Island

Aemilian bridge

CAPITOLINE HILL

Forum

Via Aurelia

TRANSTIBERIM

PALATINE HILL

JANICULUM HILL

Sublician bridge

Circus Maximus

River Tiber

AVENTINE HILL

Emporium

Porta Raudusculana

Mons Testaceus

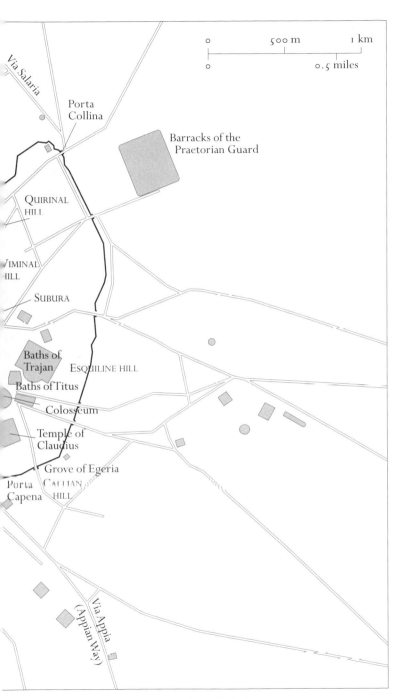

Via Salaria

Porta
Collina

Barracks of the
Praetorian Guard

QUIRINAL
HILL

VIMINAL
HILL

SUBURA

Baths of
Trajan   ESQUILINE HILL

Baths of Titus

Colosseum

Temple of
Claudius

Grove of Egeria

Porta   CAELIAN
Capena   HILL

Via Appia
(Appian Way)

500 m   1 km

0.5 miles

USEFUL PHRASES

Quidquid latine dictum sit, altum videtur
Whatever is said in Latin sounds
profound

In the bar

Quo usque tandem expectem? How long
must I wait?

Vel vinum mihi da, vel nummos mihi redde
I want my wine or my money back

*Vinum bellum iucundumque est, sed animo
corporeque caret* It's a nice little wine, but
it lacks character and depth

Da mihi fermentum Give me a beer

Ad multos annos! Cheers!

In vino veritas Truth is in wine

Ecce hora! Look at the time!

Dating

Ubi sunt puellae/pueri? Where are the
girls/boys?

Nomen mihi est Livia. Salve! Hi! My
name's Livia

Scorpio sum – quod signum tibi es?
I'm a Scorpio, what sign are you?

Estne pugio in tunica, an tibi libet me videre?
Is that a dagger in your tunic, or are you
pleased to see me?

Siren improba Wicked temptress

Nocte quater Four times a night

Magna cum voluptate With great pleasure

Volo, non valeo I want to, but I can't

Noli me tangere Get your hands off me

Re vera, cara mea, mihi nil refert Frankly my
dear, I don't give a damn

Spero nos familiares mansuros I hope we
can still remain friends

Noli me vocare, ego te vocabo Don't call
me, I'll call you

Hora et triginta minuta in mora es You are
an hour and a half late

Nescio quid dicas I don't know what
you're talking about

Errare humanum est To err is human

Lapsus linguae erat It was a slip of the
tongue

Anguis in herba es You are a snake in the
grass

Vade retro! Go away!

In the market

Pecuniam mihi monstra Show me the
money

Quantum est? How much is that?

Hoc est nimis! It's too expensive!

Caveat emptor Watch what you buy

Pecuniam mihi redde Give me back my
money

Do ut des? What do I get for that?

Hoc affer tecum Take it with you

In hac tunica obesa videbor? Do I look fat
in this tunic?

Vestis virum reddit Clothes make the man

Nonnullis desunt Some bits are missing

Pistrix rapax Greedy shark

Domestic harmony

Cara, domi adsum I'm home, darling

Fabricare diem Make my day

Non possum reminiscere I can't remember

In flagrante delicto Caught red-handed

Credo absurdum est I think that's
ridiculous

Meeting strangers

Neutiquam erro I'm not lost

Demum veniunt gladiatores Ah, the gladiators at last

Mihi ignosce Excuse me

Auxilium mihi, si placet Can you help me, please?

Quod in abysso dices? What the hell are you talking about?

Non me rape si tibi placet Please don't rob me

Noli me necare, cape omnias pecunias meas Don't kill me, here's all my money

Ubi sum? Where am I?

Quis annus est? What year is it?

Volo domum redire I want to go home

Accommodation

Ubi vales, ibi patria est Where you feel good, you feel at home

Tectum rimosum est The roof leaks

Conclave meum est flagrans My room is on fire

Ante cenam Before dinner

Cave canem Beware of the dog

Utrum per diem an per horam? Is that by the day or by the hour?

Estne juxtim caupona? Is there a tavern nearby?

Volo cum praetore expostulare I want to complain to the praetor

Being polite

Pace tua With your permission

Extemplo At once

Eheu! Mea culpa Oops! My fault

Manus manum lavat I'll help you if you help me

Diis aliter visum The gods decided otherwise

Ex animo Sincerely

De minimis non curo It's too trivial to bother me

General expressions

In quanam parte templum Iovis est? Where is the temple of Jupiter?

Ursus perpauli cerebri sum I am a bear of very little brain

Britanni ite domum Britons go home

Utinam tuus currus deleatur May your chariot be wrecked

Fortasse, haec olim meminisse nobis juvabit Perhaps we'll look back at this one day and smile

O tempora, o mores! Oh the times, the morality!

Quo vadis? Where are you going?

Scisne quo modo haec facies? Do you know how to do this?

Delirant isti Romani These Romans are crazy

Tempora mutantur et nos mutamur in illis The times change and we change with them

Haec omnia? Is that all?

Vade in pace Go in peace

Res Romae cognosco I know things about Rome

AUTHOR'S NOTE

The setting for this guide is Rome in about AD 200, but it draws on sources ranging over 300 years. I'd like to thank Dr Jim Aitken for his help with the Latin translations, and Dr Joanne Berry and Nicholas Purcell for their comments and advice, which in no way makes them guilty of the end product. I'd also like to dedicate this book to those inveterate travellers Pete and Judy, who would go there if they could. All quotations are the author's own translations. Some quotations are followed by the abbreviation *CIL*, which stands for *Corpus Inscriptionum Latinarum* – a comprehensive collection of all Latin inscriptions.

SOURCES OF ILLUSTRATIONS

© Altair4 Multimedia Roma – www.altair4.it Plates I–XI (pp. 49, 50–51, 52, 53, 54–55, 56, 105, 106–107, 108–109, 110, 111, 112);
After Boethius, A., & Ward-Perkins, J. B., *Etruscan and Roman Architecture* (London, 1970) 32;
British Museum 1, 89, 118;
© Roger Wood/CORBIS 83;
D. Stredder Bist 37;
Deutsches Museum, Munich 18;
Photo Ray Gardner 123;
from Chaillet, G., *Dans La Rome des Césars* (© Editions Glénat, 2004) 11, 81;
The Metropolitan Museum of Art, New York 45;
Museo Aquilano. Photo Alinari 21;
Museo dei Conservatori, Rome 113;
Museo Nazionale Archeologico, Naples. Photo Alinari 91;
Museo Nazionale, Portogruaro 77;
Museo Nuovo del Palazzo dei Conservatori. Photo Alinari 2;
Museo Torlonia, Rome. Photo Deutsches Archaeologisches Institut, Rome 9;
Ostia Museum. Photo Fototeca Unione 65;
Drazen Tomic 27, 59, 100, 136–137; from Tucker, T. G., *Life in the Roman World of Nero and St. Paul* (London, 1910) 35, 41, 44, 87, 117, 125;
www.forumancientcoins.com 66;
Philip Winton 133

All other line drawings are by Drazen Tomic.

The coin illustrated on the half-title page is a silver denarius.

INDEX

Page numbers in *italics* indicate in-text illustrations; colour plates are denoted by Roman numerals.

INDEX

First published in 2007 in hardcover in the United States of America by Thames & Hudson Inc., 500 Fifth Avenue, New York, New York 10110

thamesandhudsonusa.com

First paperback edition, with corrections, 2008

Library of Congress Catalog Card Number 2006907808

ISBN 978-0-500-28760-6

Printed and bound in China by SNP Leefung Printers Limited